OLLIE

The Ollie Butler Story

DAVID KNISS

ISBN: 1-4033-7859-2 (E-book)
ISBN: 1-4033-7860-6 (Paperback)

This book is printed on acid free paper.

1stBooks – rev. 04/09/03

For Ollie, his players, his family and his friends.

FOREWORD

If you don't know Ollie Butler and don't have much interest in basketball or care anything about revisiting high school, you will still be struck by this story. It is a story of America, of growing up poor and following your dreams, of the tragedy of war, of experiencing college, of moving West, of a small growing town in the Mojave Desert, of coaching basketball, of battling racism, of teaching high school history, of personal loss and overcoming adversity.

When David Kniss asked me to write the foreword for this book, I wasn't sure I was the right person for the job. It is an understatement to say that there are many people who have been closer to Ollie Butler and the basketball program at Victor Valley High School than I have. Nevertheless, as someone who started his teaching career at VVHS and taught there for sixteen years, I know most of the central characters in this dramatic story.

Julian Weaver, the principal during the most climactic and tumultuous moments in Ollie's career, and who appeared to be Ollie's nemesis during the fallout from the tournament game in Moreno Valley that would end Ollie's tenure as a high school basketball coach, was the man who hired me as a language arts teacher in 1985. I came into a school that had been ravaged by an unsuccessful strike the year before, creating bitter feelings and dividing the staff from the administration and even staff members from each other. In retrospect, the Ollie Butler incident was an addendum to that bitterness. As Julian Weaver was attacked for his handling of Ollie's case, it seemed to be a continuation of the contract-strike issue. At the time, I felt sympathy for a principal who I saw standing more and more alone as he faced off against a popular teacher and coach, and against a school community that was already angry about what it felt was an unjust administration. I saw Julian as a genuine and human character caught up in a tragedy that was not necessarily of his own making. In the end though, it wasn't Julian, the School Board, Ollie, or the CIF that would close out Ollie's career.

As for Ollie, I remember him most simply as a colleague. I attended some basketball games as a new teacher, but oftentimes I was too busy in those first couple of years to see much beyond my nose, as they say. One of my most vivid memories of him was a very commonplace one. He stopped me as we were passing in the hallway to ask me about having to sub for other teachers during prep-period. Was I being called on as much as he was? He needed that prep period time "desperately," he told me. Not to make too big a deal of this, but it meant something to have an established teacher and coach make an effort to connect with me as a peer, even if just for a minute. He probably knew that as a new teacher I could understand the feeling of being overworked as well as anyone, and his comments came across as in-the-trenches genuine.

I can tell you that no matter what else you might say about Ollie, he worked hard year-round.

To this day, as a teacher, I am amazed at colleagues who put so much of themselves into their teaching, coaching and other school responsibilities. They take the difficult road, not the easy one. And Ollie stuck with the difficult way for a long time when it would have been so much easier not to. My guess is that Ollie Butler coached basketball all of those years for the same reason most people do anything: because of love. Ollie Butler loved basketball, he loved his players, he loved teaching history and he followed this road as far as it would take him.

I had Ollie's son, Michael, who figures prominently in the climax of this story, in one of my first classes. I also knew the warmth of the late Willie McDonald, Butler's former player and long time colleague and assistant coach. Jackson Wong, who ended up in the wrong place at the right time and became a part of Victor Valley High School history, is a close friend of mine. Many members of Butler's basketball teams in the late Eighties made their way through my English classes.

Last but not least, I remember vividly the day that David Kniss was introduced to the English department at Victor Valley High. He spoke confidently and passionately, and I remember being impressed by his manner. Looking back, too, I remember the tremendous optimism and idealism that brought David to teaching in the first place, and how that has been tested, sometimes frustrated, and reborn in the recent months. This year he returns to teach at his alma mater, after a one year hiatus to put time into this book, with a new perspective and renewed determination. I know that as David prepares for yet another challenging year as a teacher and coach, he continues to be inspired and encouraged by the example of Ollie Butler and other teachers of a previous generation who set an example for all of us.

Stan Brown
28 July, 2002

ACKNOWLEDGMENTS

I wish to thank my editor, Stan Brown, who met with me weekly for months and months to give me feedback and the encouragement I needed to finish. Thanks also to Mike Foley, my creative writing instructor at the University of California at Riverside, for his inspiration. Thanks to my wife Billie, who gave me technical support on the computer and sixteen months of pester-free time to work. Thanks to everyone I interviewed; I tried to get you all into the story. And lastly, thanks most of all to Ollie and Sharon Butler, who opened up their home and their lives to provide me with the content for this book.

INTRODUCTION

Ollie Butler was my 11th grade American History teacher and my varsity basketball coach. He made a huge impact on me in high school, but I never knew how big until I became a teacher and coach myself.

One afternoon early in my career, after a particularly trying day in the classroom and an equally frustrating afternoon in the gym practicing with my freshman basketball team, I had a brainstorm to call Coach Butler and ask him some questions about teaching and coaching. "Come on over, Dave," he cordially invited. And over I went, spending a couple of hours talking things over.

I ended up having such a good time talking with Coach that I kept it up on and off over the course of that basketball season. I found out so much that later it dawned on me Coach's life might be worth writing a book about. I was an English teacher and I always wanted to write a book. What had kept me from it in the past was the basic problem of having nothing to say. But Butler's life—that would make a story worth reading. I wouldn't have to be particularly creative, all I would have to do was write down what he told me.

So I approached Coach with the idea. He seemed amused, but he agreed.

I wrote this book for three reasons. First, as a tribute to Ollie Butler. Second, for the people in my community who knew Ollie Butler as a teacher and legendary basketball coach and would be interested in knowing more about his life. And third, I wrote this book for myself, just to see if I could do it.

And now, here it is, I did it! That doesn't mean I think it's great literature or anything.

This is a regional book which chronicles Butler's 35 years as a high school basketball coach and history teacher, primarily at Victor Valley High in Victorville, California. Essentially, the book consists of three parts. The first part is about Butler's road to Victorville. The second part is about his years coaching and teaching at Victor Valley High School. The third part is about his life in retirement and Butler's philosophical approach to coaching.

The hardest part of writing this book was corroborating all the facts. Most of what I got came from long Sunday afternoon interviews with Coach in his living room. Since he's got such a sharp mind, most of his facts were accurate to the minute, day, week, month and year. Still, no one can remember everything; there were a few fuzzy areas where he was not quite sure about past events. These were the problem parts of the book for me. But rather than spend the rest of my life trying to authenticate the gaps, I gave myself 16 months to gather as much information as I could and write about what I'd discovered in that time. Ollie, of course, thought I should spend thirty years writing his biography and make it my life's work. I love him dearly but that was out of the question.

What that means is this isn't biography in the pure sense. It's a story where fact and legend meet. It's interwoven with local anecdotal history, hearsay, newspaper accounts, first and second person interviews, Coach Butler's memories, and a little creative nonfiction to bind it all together.

Finally, forget everything your high school English teacher taught you. Those school- marms were too constrained by the rules. I want to entertain you, not bore you to death. I'm going to talk to you, ask you questions and do my best to draw you right in to this story about the life of Ollie Butler.

THE BOY FROM TENNESSEE

Ollie Butler was born November 26, 1930, in Bemis, Tennessee, a little cotton-mill town 12 miles outside of Jackson, the seat of Madison County, about mid-way between Memphis and Nashville. In Tennessee, as in a lot of other places, it was common for boys to be named after their fathers, but Ollie's dad put a little twist on this custom. Rather than give his son his name, he gave him his initials—O. J. No one knows why his dad did this. Perhaps the name Oliver smacked too much of England's waifish Oliver Twist or maybe there were already too many boys running around with Jackson in their name—boys named after the famous Indian-fighting military folk-hero and seventh president, Andrew Jackson—who had campaigned passionately for president against John Quincy Adams on a pass through the area in 1824—or perhaps after another famous Jackson, the Civil War general, Stonewall Jackson. Whatever the reason, O. J. didn't get a name, just initials, and up until he was a senior in college he was known only by those initials, so that's how I'm going to refer to him until we get to that point in the story.

O. J.'s father, Oliver Jackson Butler, descended from an Irish line of farmers who came to America sometime between 1842-46 to escape the potato famine. For nearly a hundred years in America this branch of the Butler family languished in generational poverty and by the time O. J. was born the closest Oliver Jackson Butler had ever come to making any consistent money was the regular paycheck he received while fighting in World War I, known then as "The Great War." Upon discharge, he even received a cash settlement from the military, reparations for a gunshot wound in the leg that hobbled him for the rest of his life. Nowadays you'd get permanent disability. Not then. Instead, Oliver Jackson Butler got a lump sum payout and a "Good luck" handshake from Uncle Sam. He was fortunate to survive the war with only a gunshot wound, his brother-in-law had it worse. He'd inhaled Mustard gas in the trenches fighting the Germans, which ruined his lungs and brought on early heart disease.

Returning from the war partially crippled, O. J.'s father worked hard to lead a semblance of a normal life. As a boy, O. J. didn't really understand how the war had irreparably affected his father. His dad limped. His dad was quiet. And like most veterans his dad didn't talk much about being in the war. But as O. J. grew up and eventually overheard relatives whispering about the horrors of war his dad endured, he began to figure out the nature of his father's reserve. As he began to comprehend the ways of the world, these stories made a tremendous impact on him and helped him to better understand his father.

Oliver Jackson Butler was a strong moral man, honest, hard working, loyal and generous with what little he had. He had an 11th grade education and believed in the proverb, "If you can't say something good about someone, don't say anything at all." His father didn't engage in gossip. He didn't get emotional or mad either.

"I can't remember my father ever raising his voice in anger, except once," Butler recalled. O. J. had just turned eleven when he overheard a heated family conversation.

"I'm going to join the Army Air Corps," O. J.'s eldest brother James announced soon after the bombing of Pearl Harbor. Dad was for it. Mom was against it. They argued back and forth in the kitchen with James for hours. O. J. and his brothers eavesdropped from the next room.

Dad saw the military as a way out of poverty for James. The hard times of the Depression era were lingering and there was no American Charles Dickens to champion the cause of the nation's poor—although Steinbeck, with his *Grapes of Wrath,* was giving it his best shot. Oliver Jackson knew the Army Air Corps would give James career training while feeding, clothing and paying him.

Mom saw it differently. She, too, had lived through the atrocities of war many a night, vicariously, as Oliver Jackson thrashed about in the throes of nightmares—what we now know as post-traumatic-stress-syndrome. A devoutly religious woman, she wanted no part of sending a son to some faraway land to kill other mothers' sons or end up dead himself.

Oliver Jackson, in order to be fair and not hold back anything from James, revealed the horror and revulsion of his own personal experiences in The Great War that night. For the first time in his life, O. J. heard his dad get loud and emotional. Young James had a romantic vision of the military and his father did not want him looking at enlistment through rose-colored glasses. He spilled out the brutality of what he had seen and done a half a lifetime ago while his wife sat by hoping a realistic description of war would deter James.

"It was the only time I ever remember my parents arguing," O. J. said. "Me and my younger brothers heard everything, and surprisingly, after it was all said and done, Mom relented. James joined the Army Air Corps with both Mom and Dad's blessing."

The normal life that Oliver Jackson pursued: marriage, work and supporting a family of seven children, was never easy. The war had ruined him physically. He would never be full-strength again and it was impossible for him to hide his limp. Because of this disability he had a hard time getting good jobs. For a few years after he returned from the Great War he worked as an itinerant farmer for various well-to-do growers. He farmed cotton, tomatoes, corn, peanuts and various other crops, though never tobacco. He walked the gravel roads to work where he labored long hours to make what little wages were available but he never earned more than a subsistence for his family. He was a lowly sharecropper, and "Sharecropping," as Robert Gordon says in his book about Muddy Waters, "is about getting less than half of what you got coming to you."

O. J. remembers working as a young boy in the fields with his brothers to help bring in extra money. "We crawled up and down between the furrows with sacks tied to our belts picking cotton balls until our hands bled." O. J. didn't care for this manual labor nor did he have much of an aptitude for it either. Even when he was promoted and given a plow to use, he still wasn't much of a farmer. "I plowed the crookedest furrows in all of Tennessee."

Times were tough in the Thirties. Roosevelt's relief programs weren't making much of an impact in Bemis to relieve the suffering of the poor. O. J. felt an uncanny distress well up inside of him as he crawled up and down the dirt furrows of other men's farm fields. *Why are we poor? Why does Dad have to work so hard? How are we ever going to escape this mean, shabby, insignificant existence?* That's when O. J. Butler had his first epiphany.

Sleeping out under the stars one night, O. J. contemplated his future, a rare thing in a young boy. From the sublime heavens he gathered in solace. Awareness. It was as if the stars were influencing his thoughts. This groveling in the dirt was not for him. He did not want to follow in his father's footsteps. There had to be something better. He wasn't exactly sure what it might be but he determined to figure it out.

O. J.'s mother, Stella May Sanders Butler, was a barely literate second grade dropout who left school at eight when her mother died in order to help care for her siblings. Born in 1900, she lived to be 82, dying in 1982 from complications from diabetes. "Mama didn't talk about herself," Butler said. "What little I know for sure about her background came from my sister Emma Lou. Her real name was Emily, but we never called her Emily. She was a straight A student in school and the family historian. To tease her, we called her Scarlet O'Butler."

Stella May was a big proponent of education for her own children. She knew what it felt like to be unschooled, though ironically, her ancestors were rumored to have been educated aristocratic plantation owners in the early 19th century who had lost their property following the Civil War. O. J. remembers that although his mother may have been uneducated, "She wrote to me regularly while I was in the Air Force and in college. Her letters were a little hard to read because of her spelling, but they had a

3

wonderful spirit to them." She was also the one who encouraged him to learn as much as he could in school.

O. J. was the fourth of seven children. He grew up scrappy and tenacious—a trademark of many middle children from large families desperately trying to avoid getting lost in the pack. O. J. learned early, if you don't assert yourself, you're going to be overlooked. This wasn't for him. He liked the limelight too much.

As you can imagine, poverty was tough on the Butler family. Since sharecroppers got by mostly on trade they had virtually no cash money. They were always in debt until the next crop came in. Luxuries were nonexistent. In especially lean times the Butler children verged on malnourishment. Too often they went to school hungry, improperly attired and without basic school supplies like notebooks, paper and writing instruments. Neither did they have any type of regular medical or dental care. Their saving grace in times of medical emergencies was that their good-hearted country doctor still made house calls and didn't mind taking payment in trade if folks couldn't afford to pay with money.

Being poor, little pleasures were big to O. J. "Free school lunches were the best thing going," Butler reminisced. "I would trade just about anything to get a second helping of cafeteria rice pudding with raisins."

Up until O. J. went to high school, the family lived in accommodations provided by the farm owners his father worked for. Today we'd consider them shacks or shanties, barely habitable; to O. J. each one was home. Though they had no indoor plumbing, gas heating, electric lighting, or telephone, they provided a roof overhead and shelter from the elements. "If there was a water pump close by," Butler said, "we considered ourselves fortunate. You have no idea how hard times were then."

An automobile was a luxury they dreamed not of. A horse was beyond consideration as well. Between nine of them they had one bicycle. Butler remembers, "Walking was a way of life."

Bemis had a small population, about 3500, but it was close to the much larger city of Jackson, population 50,000. (In the 1980s Bemis was absorbed by the city of Jackson, urban sprawl and all that, and exists now only as an historical site within Jackson.) Jackson inspired O. J. The hustle and bustle he saw there on his rare excursions to the city gave him a glimpse of a better life. The streets were paved. Average people lived in nice houses, drove automobiles, ate in restaurants and shopped in department stores. What he saw opened his eyes further to the idea that there was more to life than the impoverished existence he was currently living. O. J. went to Jackson whenever he could.

Bemis, on the other hand, wasn't exactly what you'd call inspiring. Oppressive would describe it better. It was a "Company Town" run by the

Bemis Brothers Bag Company (specializing in sacks used for bagging cotton and other crops). The Bemis Brothers owned all the local real estate so you had to rent from them if you lived in the town limits. They also owned the only store. You bought all your food and supplies from them because they would extend you credit if you were short of cash. This turned into a pattern of economic bondage that was hard to escape. A man would cash his paycheck at the store then have to pay off all the charges he'd made on account, leaving little left over for savings. Within a week or two the cycle of borrowing against next month's wages began again. The working class was thereby kept in a state of perpetual dependency. It was a vicious struggle for survival, especially in the depths of the Depression, and for the sons of poor European immigrants who'd come to this area looking for a better way of life in America, the "good life" was slow in developing. However, where the youngsters were concerned, childhood had a way of finding a silver lining in the dark clouds of reality.

Bemis had a new YMCA and O. J. and his friends loved going there. "There was a gym," Butler recalled, "recreation rooms with a pool table and a ping-pong table, tennis courts, a couple of regulation softball fields, and all of it was surrounded by verdant lawns." The "Y" was open to all boys who followed Forrest Brook's rules of behavior. Brooks was the YMCA supervisor.

"Brooks didn't allow any swearing," Butler remembered, "and he always reminded us to act as if our mother were watching." Brooks was a strong role-model to the boys of Bemis. Years later, as a teacher and coach himself, Butler, too, continued the practice of speaking decently and respectfully. He didn't allow swearing or cursing in his classroom or on the basketball court either.

Another bright spot in Butler's grim Depression-era childhood was the movies, also known as "the talkies" or "the picture show." An indelible memory associated with one particular film has stuck with Butler since the first grade and goes as follows: "One cool Saturday afternoon in early December, my brother James and I went to see Robert Taylor in, "Johnny Eager." I'll never forget it because I had just turned eight years old. For some reason we both had the particular good fortune to have a quarter each. In those days you could get into the movies for a dime. A coke and a popcorn cost a nickel a piece. That left a nickel for after the movies to buy an ice-cream, always a Big Nick [similar to a Sidewalk Sundae]. We watched the movie and stayed after it ended to watch part of it again. You could do that then. Movies always started over again right after they ended. I guess they did that so in case anyone came in late they could still see what they missed, that is unless you came late to the last show of the night. Anyway, we came out after dark, just before the ice-cream parlor closed.

We got our Big Nick and sat down on the curb to eat it. By the time we finished it was pitch black. We'd ridden over in the afternoon on the family bicycle. Well, James was pretty smart, he'd brought along a flashlight. He handed it to me. I jumped up on the handlebars and away we went with me shining the light to guide the way."

O. J. GOES TO SCHOOL

O. J. began school later than most kids. Why? He missed the cut off day. He was born in November and back then if you weren't seven by September 1, you had to wait until the following year to start school. Most of his friends were a little older and went on to school that year without him. Luckily, when he caught up to them at school the next year, some of his buddies had flunked first grade and were there to welcome him.

When he finally entered the first grade he found out being one of the older kids in the class had some advantages. O. J. was more aware than his younger classmates. His savvy helped to compensate for his lack of size in the schoolyard pecking order. He knew enough to keep out of the way of "rounders"—juvenile delinquents like his older brother John William. In primary school his teachers praised his imagination and creativity. The extra year he had on most of his classmates gave him a mental edge in gaining the teacher's attention.

Unlike many boys his age, O. J. loved school. He did well in his studies too, at least throughout primary and elementary school. His mom was especially proud of his progress because he served as a positive role-model to his younger brothers, in contrast to their older brother, John William—the rounder. But needless to say, O. J.'s love of school eventually waned. By the time he'd moved into the sixth grade he wasn't nearly as keen on school as he once was. Some of that might have had to do with his sixth grade teacher, Mrs. Hicks. After all, numerous studies since then have shown that the most important factor in student achievement and motivation is the teacher.

"Mrs. Hicks was a devout Southern Baptist and she didn't have a funny-bone. She was very strict and puritanical," Butler recalls. A scene etched into his sixth grade experience with Mrs. Hicks may serve to characterize her better: "Mrs. Hicks loved to work Christianity into the curriculum whenever she could. One thing she would do every Monday was ask who had gone to Sunday school. She made us give her a show of hands. Even though most of us did not go to church we all usually raised our hands. After counting our hands she would recite a Bible verse, then ask if any of us could recite one. My mom was Pentecostal and she didn't take me to church that often so I didn't know very many verses. I always felt uncomfortable about this. Some of my friends did too. Well, one day someone got the idea that we could annoy Mrs. Hicks if we all started reciting the shortest verses we could think of. It became a secret competition that one boy won when he quoted, 'Jesus wept.' When Mrs. Hicks caught on to our game she got pretty mad."

In the eighth grade O. J. came to a crossroads in his academic career. "I hit the wall, as they say, and brought home 12 U's [U=unsatisfactory]: six in deportment and six in academics." His eighth grade teacher went to work on him and did everything she could to turn him around—including physical coercion such as pulling his ear, tweaking his nose, breaking more than a ruler or two over his knuckles, and even spankings. But as any amateur psychologist can tell you, fear of punishment only works temporarily. A positive rather than a negative incentive works much better when it comes to motivation. Ultimately O. J. found his own incentive in sports. In order to play high school ball he had to return to the fold of sound academics and good citizenship in order to be eligible for the team.

HIGH SCHOOL SPORTS

Like most ordinary boys his age, O. J. loved outdoor sports and by the time he hit high school he was already well-regarded amongst his peers as a standout athlete. You know the kind of kid, either he was the one who the other boys wanted to be captain and chose up fair teams or he was the kid that any other captain would always pick first.

O. J.'s first love was baseball. He played it every chance he got. When his younger brothers were small and didn't know any better, he really had it made. He convinced Lewis, Larry and Ray that fielding and throwing were the most important aspects of the game, allowing him to do all the hitting necessary to build their fielding skills. He would hit them balls for hours. The extra hitting paid off for O. J. He became such a good placement hitter that he was recruited by the town's men's team in his early teens. All the fielding practice paid off for younger brother Ray, too, who ended up being such a strong fielding catcher that he led his team to the Little League World Series in Williamsport, Pennsylvania. Don't ask. They lost.

O. J.'s devotion to baseball is replete with anecdotes. He played baseball year round, and when they weren't playing it they were listening to it on the radio. Too poor to afford to go and see a professional game, they lived for radio broadcasts and the occasional free minor-league exhibition game.

One particular exhibition game that Butler told me about might still interest boys today. I quote the story in its entirety: "There was a professional exhibition game going to be played nearby and my friends and I wanted to go see it, but the game was at 1:00 p.m. and we had school. We put our heads together a while and decided the only solution was to play hookey. Instead of going to school that day we hitch-hiked into Milan to the ball park. The game was terrific—especially with the element of delinquency surrounding our absence from school. The next day our principal, Mr. Raines, who was also the coach of our school basketball team, called us into the office to ask us about our coincidental absences (three friends all out on the same day). We thought Mr. Raines, a baseball enthusiast himself, would understand if we simply told the truth, so out we came with our confession. We told him about the hitch-hiking, the thrill of the game, the attempt to get autographs from the players afterwards and the pride we felt in our initiative. Surely he understood. And understood he did. He told us that he knew how great the temptation must have been for boys our age; he also told us that for every action there was a reaction and consequence. The consequence for our cutting school would be him giving us ten swats each. Now I had the misfortune to be called in last to get my swats, which meant I had to sit outside Raines' office and listen to my two friends receive theirs first. I winced with each of their cries, anticipating my own sore backside. Finally, after what seemed like an eternity, it was my turn to enter the den of doom. The paddle shone with the glow of worn denim rubbed off the backsides of my fellow rapscallions. It had the words 'Board of Education' printed on it and the paddle part was at least a foot long with a handle nearly the same length and holes had been drilled throughout the paddle to allow airflow for a better disciplinary wind-up. The swats drew blood for each boy. When it was all over, I couldn't sit down comfortably for about five days but I managed to keep from crying. That was the last time I ever received a paddling and it was also the last time I ever ditched school; but it didn't dim my love for baseball one iota."

Each summer O. J. played sandlot baseball (Little League hadn't arrived yet!) until he was old enough to play American Legion baseball. By then, he and his pal Floyd Martin were so good they also played on the town's men's team. Butler was a standout base-hitter, defenseman and base-stealer. Like Ty Cobb, Butler loved to steal home whenever the opportunity presented itself.

When Butler started high school as a freshman at J. B. Young he was quickly disappointed when he found out there was only one sport he could play. He would have liked to play football and baseball but competitive baseball and football hadn't come to J. B. Young High School yet. The only competitive sport the school sponsored was basketball. So Butler tried out for the basketball team. He was a gifted athlete, but he really hadn't played much basketball up to that point. If it weren't for the coach's loyalty to some of the returning seniors, O. J. probably would have made the team despite his lack of fundamentals; instead, he was the last player cut. The coach told O. J. he wanted to keep him but he didn't have the heart to cut one of the seniors who'd been on the team the last couple years.

O. J. didn't like being cut, last man or not, so he practiced hard in the off season and the next year he made the varsity basketball team easily; unfortunately for the J. B. Young Cats (their mascot was a cat climbing out of a Bemis Bag Company cotton sack), O. J. made the team at another school.

In the summer preceding O. J.'s sophomore year, his father took a job in Gibson, twenty miles down the road from Bemis, forcing O. J. to transfer to Gibson High. O. J. played at Gibson for two years. He started on the varsity his sophomore and junior years in both basketball and baseball. On both teams he was one of the best players. He ended up the second leading scorer on the basketball team his sophomore year and the leading scorer his junior year. In baseball he was voted by his peers the team's best all-around player both seasons.

In the summer, following his sophomore year at Gibson, O. J. had the chance to return to J. B. Young High. Again, his father had changed jobs. The new job took him and the family to Cedar Grove, just across the highway from Bemis. This was a great move for the family as it secured them their first house with electricity. However, O. J. had done so well his sophomore year that he didn't want to leave Gibson. His coaches and new friends didn't want him to leave either. It was arranged that O. J. would stay and live with a succession of families two weeks at a time. His entire junior year was spent as a vagabond, picking up and moving at the end of each bi-weekly period to live with a different teammate. This was done because folks were so poor that no one family could afford an extra boarder for a whole year. It also shows you how well O. J. was thought of that a whole group of people would be willing to go to the extra expense and imposition to keep him around (no different, I suppose, than Mater Dei giving scholarships to poor seven foot centers). By the end of his highly successful junior year, the folks of Gibson had arranged for Butler to live with one well-to-do family his entire senior year. That wouldn't happen. Butler was homesick for his own family and returned to live with them. He would finish high school where he had begun, at J. B. Young in Bemis.

O. J. was welcomed home with open arms. His old friends were glad to have him back and playing with them rather than against them. Butler had an excellent senior year. The basketball team had one of J. B. Young's best seasons ever in 1948-49, they went 22-5. Strangely, the five games they lost were to two teams. Three times they lost to Humbolt with their All-American Doug Atkins—who went on to play football at Tennessee and then into the NFL as a tight-end for the Chicago Bears. The other two losses were to big city powerhouse Jackson High. O. J. led his basketball team in scoring, assists and steals. On the American Legion baseball team, he was voted the best all-around player just like he was at Gibson. His baseball team didn't do as well as the basketball team, but O. J. put up great numbers individually. He hit near .400, and led the team in RBI's and stolen bases.

Butler wasn't too shabby in the classroom either. He got outstanding grades (A's and B's) all through high school. He didn't date. (He says he was too shy.) He worked part-time when he could and focused on academics and sports the rest of the time. And by the end of his senior year, he was ready to take a shot at pro baseball.

Upon graduating high school, that now classical American right of passage, O. J. intended to try out for and make a professional minor league baseball team and work his way up to the big leagues. This was how he planned to transcend the narrow margin of his family's impoverished life. He would be the one to break the generational bonds of poverty and put his folks on easy street in their senior years. He had earned recognition and acclaim in the Bemis and Gibson area as an athlete. He was the town's brightest star. He was known to the athletes of Jackson as their fiercest competitor. Many of the locals were confident he would make a minor league team when he tried out; after all, hadn't he been leading the men's team for the past four years in hitting and base-stealing. Just read the papers. Hadn't he been a high school superstar. He was locally famous. He was also a good student and a young gentleman. He had been a perfect role model ever since his hookey incident. Everything was working in his favor. He'd prepared himself for this opportunity. He knew he could do this!

Unfortunately, when he tried out for the Mayfield, Kentucky Class D team, the scouts didn't see him the same way his townsmen did. Sure the kid could hit, but he had no power. Sure he could field, but he didn't have great arm strength. True, he was quick on the base-pads, but at five foot ten inches and 130 pounds, the scouts told him, he was way too small.

And that was that. He could try out again next year if he wanted.

Embarrassed by not making the team, Butler wondered what to do next. He walked home in order to think it through. How would he avoid a life of digging in the dirt if he stuck around Bemis? There weren't too many options. It was either farming or the Bag Company. That is until he saw Harold West slide a Help Wanted sign into his store window. The next day Butler began work as a soda jerk at West's Pharmacy—to him it beat farming or making cotton sacks.

U. S. AIR FORCE

In 1950, Uncle Sam issued a stentorian bugle call of esprit de corps to the young men of America. Democracy was again under attack, this time at the 38th parallel. China was the newest threat. In the wake of the recently ended World War II effort that had drawn America patriotically together and pulled us out of the Great Depression, there was still an underlying feeling permeating the country that the world was not yet truly safe. The U. S. Air Force was the newest branch of the United States military, having been founded on September 18,1947, and when O. J. saw their recruiters in town, he got curious.

Communism was the latest threat to world security. Wherever it encroached, our political soothsayers decried, democracy was at risk. Russia, too, was a concern, but even more ominous was the Chinese Communist Party, a totalitarian regime under the control of Mao Zedong. Following the Allied Powers' defeat of imperialistic Japan, Zedong led his red army to a coup over his more democratic rival, Chiang K'ai-shek, and became chief of state of the newly formed People's Republic of China. Mao sought to build China into a modern industrial nation and sought alliance with the U.S.S.R. To the United States, the Chinese government appeared an immediate successor to the Nazi specter, and according to Uncle Sam's military point man in the East, General Douglas MacArthur, communism must be stopped on the far away Asian front between North and South Korea or a domino effect would take place, resulting in one small Southeast Asian country after another being vanquished by Mao's hobgoblin red army.

O. J. Butler, after working for a year following high school graduation making ice-cream soda's in Harold West's store, heard Uncle Sam's call to arms loud and clear. He was bored with small town living. This was an opportunity to move on. So he talked old pal Floyd Martin into signing up with him to go into the Air Force. The clarion call to duty by his country had also gotten him thinking about his future. If the pro baseball scouts thought he was too small, he could go into the military and build himself up. With the training and drilling and regimentation of the service, he could transform himself into a bigger, stronger fellow. By the time he was discharged, he figured, he would be a physical specimen of iron muscle, cat-like agility, and Sherpa endurance. When he again tried out for a professional baseball team, no scout would dare call him puny. Furthermore, like WWII hero Audie Murphy, Butler fantasized that in fighting the good fight for democracy in Korea he might even possibly return home a war hero. How could a pro baseball scout turn down a well built veteran war hero? These were the grandiose thoughts of a green recruit with a new dream. He couldn't have been more idealistic than Henry Fleming entering the Civil War in <u>The Red Badge of Courage</u>.

On August 13, 1950, Butler and Martin went to Jackson to enlist. Basic training took them to Lackland Air Force Base in San Antonio, Texas. On the train trip from Jackson to San Antonio, the sergeant selected Butler to oversee the new recruits. Why Butler? He asked himself the same question. The only reason he could figure was that he was older. Almost all the boys on the train had just graduated high school that summer, but he was almost 20 and had been out of school a whole year giving him an extra year of worldly experience and sophistication. From San Antonio a bus took them the rest of the way to Lackland. Butler remembered that a lot of the boys really weren't ready for what they were getting into. "That first night in the barracks," he said, "I never heard so much crying in my life!"

O. J.'s three month Basic Training initiation into the machinations of military life was gratifying, much to the disbelief of his fellow recruits. Coming from a background of poverty, O. J. loved the three abundant mess-hall meals he received each day. "The best part about those meals," Butler recalled, "was you could eat as much as you wanted in the allotted time. Remember, I was essentially malnourished as a kid. For me, the mess-hall was a daily Thanksgiving banquet."

O. J. also loved the barracks atmosphere and the team-like camaraderie of drilling and training. It was a lot like the discipline of being on the varsity basketball or baseball team, except here he got paid for his workout. His friends couldn't believe his attitude. They constantly grumbled and whined. On the contrary, Butler couldn't understand their complaining. He thought this new life was just about the greatest. He drew a pay check every month of $75, a windfall of wealth he had never known before. His room and board were paid for. Regular medical and dental attentions were as good as an additional stipend. "I'd grown up without any type of regular health care. In the Air Force, I was finally able to get some long neglected dental work done that my folks could never afford."

The Air Force, Butler acknowledges, was not heaven, but in comparison to his privations and hardships back home it was a far cry from the hell many of the other recruits claimed it to be. The Air Force took care of his material needs and creature comforts better than they had ever been taken care of before. He didn't feel like he was missing anything. He didn't feel lonely or deprived of some familiar way of life the way a lot of the other fellas seemed to. While they were drinking in bars or visiting the local whore houses, Butler would visit the public library, check out any local museums, play some pick up ball at the YMCA, or go to the movies.

Basic training at Lackland was succeeded by eight more months of technical training in Camp Gordon, Georgia. They didn't take the train or a bus to get there though, they flew, and that's when Butler found out he didn't like flying—he got horribly air sick. To this day Butler won't fly if he can avoid it. He'd rather drive for 13 hours to see his kids in Denver than get in a plane and be there in two hours.

At Camp Gordon, O. J. was educated in the field of radio repair. "It wasn't a job I would have picked," Butler stated, "it was a job the Air Force picked for me based on an aptitude test I took. Personally, I didn't think I was very mechanically inclined." And then Butler pulls my leg a little to tease me about his ineptness, "Heck, just last month I called the Water Company to see why the hot water wasn't coming out of the faucet."

While completing radio repair school at Camp Gordon, Butler received the sad news that his older brother James, who had served with honor and distinction as a staff sergeant in the old Army Air Corps during World War II and who had recently reenlisted for the Korean hostilities, had been killed in a B-29 training-flight in the Azores. B-29s were nicknamed "widow-makers" because they crashed so frequently. O. J. winced as he recalled joking with James about this in the past. O. J. returned home to comfort their mother and help his sister with funeral arrangements. He was given a month's leave.

Fate is a belief that the gods tinker with our lives and that we are subject to their whims. Destiny, on the other hand, is a theory that cause and effect rule the world. One thing leads to another and this turns out to be your destiny. What happens in your destiny can always be traced back to specific prior events. When death strikes a family unexpectedly, everyone wants to try and figure it out. Usually the bereaved give their departed friend or relative's death some sort of special significance if at all possible. The Butler's did this with James. Although his death was a tragic accident—the B-29 hit a telephone pole along the runway in the fog—James had also made the ultimate sacrifice in giving his life in the quest of upholding his country's freedom. The Butler's made sense of it this way. But for O. J., as far fetched as it may sound, James' death was the crossroads that led directly to his destiny to become a basketball coach and history teacher. Let me explain.

When O. J. returned to Camp Gordon his squadron was gone. They had been deployed to Korea in his absence. He expected the orders to join his squadron would come through quickly, so he bided his time, and, quite naturally, while he was waiting he did a little soul-searching. "My brother had just been killed. My unit had taken off for the front. When were they going to send for me? Would I get killed too? All I could do was sit and wait. Wait and see. Those were some of the longest days of my life. Life had never been so precious to me as it was following James' death. I started to hope secretly that maybe they would forget about me. I was no longer in any hurry to become a war hero."

At the end of his first week back Butler's TDY orders came. He was surprised. He wasn't joining his unit in Korea, he was being sent to Perrin Air Force Base near Sherman, Texas, to a radio repair squadron. Then, a month after arriving at Perrin, he received permanent orders; he was reassigned altogether. You'll never guess where the Air Force sent him! He was told to report to the base gym at Perrin, where he would assist the sergeant in charge with scheduling, maintenance and public relations. His radio repairman training would never be used except for occasional tinkering with the radio in the office—turning it off and on and tuning the station.

Butler believes he may have been assigned to the gym because he had tried out for and made the base's baseball team within a week after his arrival at Perrin. The military was known for taking care of its athletes and Butler quickly established himself as an extraordinary player. The colonel was a big baseball fan who faithfully watched the Perrin team play. In Butler's first game, he caught the colonel's attention with his placement hitting, his fiery style of base-running and his defense in the field.

Whatever the reason for this new job taking care of the base gym, it would be influential in Butler's destiny to become a high school basketball coach, although at the time Butler had never given coaching a single thought. He would finish out his enlistment at Perrin dust- mopping the gym floor every day. He was never sent to Korea. Eventually, the staff sergeant more or less turned over the entire operation of the gym to Butler. Butler scheduled all the practice times and tournament schedules, he supervised the open-gym hours, organized exhibition events and even learned how to launder uniforms and fold towels. He often put in overtime monitoring the open gym hours on the weekend—which earned him an extra $10 per Saturday. He did this whenever he wasn't playing in a game for the base's team.

When baseball season ended, Butler tried out for the base's basketball team, and, big surprise, he made that team too. Throughout his remaining tenure in the Air Force, Butler played six months of basketball and six months of baseball. He wasn't working, he was playing. How many guys are lucky enough to have that kind of destiny play out? Playing ball isn't usually what comes to most people's minds when they think of military service.

The Perrin teams traveled around to compete against other bases. Each base team was comprised of some of the best athletes in the country since at that time military deferments were considered unpatriotic. Great student-athletes of the day regularly chose military service over college, even if they came from rich families who knew how to get them out of their military obligations. Butler says, "I played against a number of All-Americans while at Perrin, guys who went back to school after their hitch in the service and made major college teams. A couple of the guys I played against even made the pros."

Besides competing against other bases, the military teams also played exhibition games against local men's teams and against local celebrity teams. This built goodwill with the civilian community. Often there was a cookout or dance following the games. The highlight for Butler though, came in 1952, when his Perrin basketball team played against Sheppard AFB to go to the Air Force Championship. They were 29-3 before the game. Butler had the unenviable task of guarding All-American guard, Norm Pilgrim (Oklahoma A & M). Butler had a terrific game against Pilgrim, holding him to 11 points. However, it wasn't enough, they lost 51-50 to finish 29-4.

The military made a man out of O. J. When he returned to civilian life he knew how to manage his money, organize his time and take care of his business. He was, as they say, "squared away." He had also achieved his primary goal of building up his strength, ability and stamina. He'd entered the military at about 130 pounds, but by the time of his discharge he'd put on another 10 pounds, and all 140 pounds of him was now solid muscle. But even more important than his additional brawn, O. J. had matured in his thinking. He had grown up.

As O. J. prepared to leave the service, he reflected back on his motivations for joining up in the first place. Mainly he'd wanted to get stronger so he could try out for and make a professional baseball team. Now, becoming a professional baseball player no longer held the same place in his heart as it had when he signed his enlistment papers. Actually, he'd grown fonder of basketball after all those hours in the weatherproof gym; but more than that, he'd come to realize that education was probably a more pragmatic road to future success.

With the G. I. Bill available, and with well-honed athletic skills, Butler thought he'd try his hand at college. Mel Brown, an offensive guard on the University of Oklahoma's football team, had become a friend of Butler's in the summer of '53 when they played baseball together. Brown regaled Butler with wonderful stories about college life at Oklahoma, so Butler decided to give the University of Oklahoma a try.

UNIVERSITY OF OKLAHOMA

On September 4, 1953, Butler was discharged from the Air Force. The next day he was at the University of Oklahoma knocking on the door of basketball coach Bruce Drake's office. "I walked in and asked to try out for the basketball team."

Butler went to see the basketball coach first because it was a fall sport. If he couldn't play basketball at the university he would try elsewhere. He still wanted to play baseball but that didn't start until February. He figured if he could make the basketball team, with its much smaller roster, then he would have no trouble making the baseball team when the time came, too.

Drake wasn't there, but assistant coach Shockey Needy was. He looked the five foot ten inch Butler over. Butler was the picture of health, athletic looking and as fit as he'd ever been in his life. "Tryouts are in October," replied Needy.

"I can't wait 'til October to find out. I need to know now if I can play here," Butler countered.

Needy looked hard at Butler. There was something about this brash guy that he instinctively liked. "Have you got your gym clothes and sneakers?" Needy asked.

O. J. did, so Needy took Butler to the gym and put him through an individual one-hour tryout. When it was finished, Needy nodded his head in approval and matter-of-factly said, "You will do." Butler enrolled at Oklahoma the next day.

Now, you might be thinking to yourself, this sounds a little far fetched, how do you get a tryout for a college team when you aren't enrolled in school? Good question. But remember, this was 1953 and things didn't work then like they do today.

The last thing Butler wanted at that point in time was just to go to college. No, he wanted to continue playing ball and he saw college as the best way to do that. To stay eligible for basketball and baseball he would have to go to classes. Hey, a college education would be a good thing too. If he didn't turn pro in sports, he'd have a college degree to earn a living with. So the first thing Butler had to find out before enrolling at a university was whether or not he could make their team. Being a natural born talker he figured he could talk his way into a personal tryout then let his athletic skills take care of the rest. That's just what he did.

As he and Needy walked to the gym, O. J. answered Needy's questions about playing ball in high school. Statistically Butler had done well at Gibson and J. B. Young, he had numbers worth boasting about. He was the team's scoring leader two seasons, assist leader three seasons, steal leader three seasons, and was voted the top all-around hustler at both high schools he played at. Needy also asked about O. J.'s military ball-playing. O. J. told him about the top athletes he'd competed against who had gotten out ahead of him and were already playing for colleges around the country, some of them were even playing for teams in the same conference as Oklahoma. O. J. also told him about almost playing in the Military Championship game in 1952.

The more O. J. talked the more convinced Needy became he had nothing to lose but an hour of his time. Either this guy was the biggest self-deluded windbag, or...possibly... One thing for sure, the guy had confidence. Hell, it was worth it to see if this fast talking Southerner could back up any of his braggadocio.

As Needy put Butler through a variety of shooting, ball-handling, agility and stamina drills, he was amazed. It just didn't happen like this. Never before had a veteran walked in off the street, cold, looking for a tryout the day after being discharged from the Air Force. Neither had Needy ever been talked into a personal tryout before. He knew it was a long-shot gamble, yet, the last thing he expected was the dazzling scene that unfolded.

Butler was magical with the ball. In that one hour tryout he whirled, juked, floated, faked, drove, accelerated, backpedaled, slid, dove, and shot like no other freshman recruit Needy had ever seen. It looked like this Butler kid was just what he claimed to be. Needy decided quickly, but he didn't want to let on to Butler just how impressed he had been, hence the nod, and the matter-of-fact "You will do."

Needy instructed Butler about getting installed at Lincoln House, the freshman athlete's dormitory. Needy would talk to Drake about a basketball scholarship to supplement Butler's G.I. Bill. The next day Butler registered for his classes and picked up his books. Basketball practice would begin in October but unofficial workouts would commence in the gym the following week. Just like that, Butler's transition from military to civilian life was complete.

On the advice of his counselor, Butler decided to major in education. The baby-boom was on and many new schools were already being built. As a teacher, the counselor advised, Butler could always get a job. When he graduated in 1957, he was qualified in five subject areas: science, history, English, physical education, and driver's training. Lucky for us—his students at Victor Valley High—Butler eventually settled on history. The stories he told made class fly by each day and actually interested us in the subject.

Butler didn't make Oklahoma's varsity basketball team as a freshman, but it wasn't because he wasn't good enough. In the Fifties the NCAA didn't allow freshman to play varsity. The freshman team didn't compete much against other schools either, what they did mostly was practice, drill, condition, scrimmage, and learn Drake's system so that perhaps they'd be ready for the varsity as sophomores, if not, they'd have to play JVs.

The freshmen were coached by John Grayson, another of Drake's assistants. Butler quickly became one of Grayson's favorites. "John Grayson," Butler noted, "was a great strategizer. In all my years of coaching I don't think I ever met anyone who was as good with the X's and O's as he was." Butler enjoyed playing for Grayson and he learned a lot from him, never imagining that a few years later he'd be coaching basketball with Grayson at the NCAA Division I collegiate level.

In the 1950s Oklahoma was in the Big Seven Conference. As the head coach, Bruce Drake had led the Oklahoma "Roundball Runts" to six Big Six and Big Seven titles already. Their best finish was in 1947 when they lost to Holy Cross in the NCAA finals. Drake's teams were known for their ball-control weaving offense, known as the "Drake Shuffle." Their biggest rivals then were Oklahoma A & M (now Oklahoma State), Nebraska and Texas. However, by the time O. J. Butler arrived, Oklahoma wasn't popular any longer for its basketball teams, it was known for its football and wrestling programs.

Butler was at Oklahoma during the zenith of the football team's glory and he went to all the home games. He was a big football fan though he had never played organized football himself. "I would have," he said, "but we didn't have football at our high school until the year after I graduated."

While Butler had great respect for Bruce Drake, who was near the end of his tenure at Oklahoma in 1953, Butler was more impressed by the football program's organization and coaching. Bud Wilkinson was Oklahoma's head football coach. According to O. J., who remembered observing him at some of their practices, Wilkinson was a dominant figure. He had a commanding presence, something like Walter Scott's Disinherited Knight in *Ivanhoe*. Butler also noticed that Wilkinson was a great delegator. "He'd walk all over the field twirling his whistle, nonchalantly moving from group to group overseeing what his assistants were teaching, though the only group I ever saw him actually take an active part in was the quarterback corps."

Wilkinson had been a quarterback himself, and though Butler had grown up in Tennessee and was much younger than Wilkinson, he knew of Wilkinson's renown. At the University of Minnesota, Wilkinson was famous for playing on three National Championship teams in 1934, '35 and '36. As a senior, he was repositioned from pulling guard to quarterback— an unheard of transition today—and guided his team to an undefeated season and a third consecutive title, after which he was named All-American at quarterback. More amazing than that, in 1937, following the Golden Gopher's championship season, the University of Minnesota was invited to play an exhibition game against the Green Bay Packers. For the first time ever a college team beat a professional team. Wilkinson helped engineer the 7-0 win. (Undoubtedly that's when the Packers started looking for a Vince Lombardi type to lead them out of the wilderness.)

As the head coach at Oklahoma, Wilkinson won a fourth National Championship in 1950, the same year O. J. joined the Air force. Then, while Butler was a student at Oklahoma, Wilkinson won two more National Championships in 1955 and 1956.

Now hold on a minute, I can hear you saying, why am I telling you so much about Bud Wilkinson in a book about Ollie Butler? Here's why. Even though Butler didn't play football, he learned a lot about coaching, leadership and building a program's tradition by watching what Wilkinson did at Oklahoma.

"He was a big man," Butler recalls, "almost regal in his bearing. He filled up a room with his presence. He exuded confidence. I'm pretty sure he had a background in literature as he was a very eloquent speaker. He reminded me of some of the generals I'd seen in the Air Force. He made a huge impression on me. I liked his demeanor and knew I wanted to learn to carry myself the way he did."

Butler loved going to Oklahoma football games with his best friend Ed Abbey. They played together on the freshman basketball team. Abbey, who was six foot five inches tall, was rather slow. O. J. used to rib him by saying, "Abbey, you're so slow you can only celebrate Christmas every other year." However, Abbey compensated for his slow foot-speed by having a fast car. His father was a wealthy automobile dealer in Denver who each year gave his son the choice of the latest model. This year Ed Abbey had a brand new convertible Thunderbird.

Butler lit up as we sat in his comfortable living room one Sunday afternoon watching the Denver Broncos light up the San Diego Chargers while talking about his college days. His favorite adventure with Abbey was their memorable road-trip to watch Oklahoma play Texas in the Red River rivalry game held in Dallas. (Texas University always played that game in centralized Dallas so more Texas fans could attend, though that year Butler thought there were more fans there for Oklahoma.) "Oklahoma had a huge fan following. You can't believe how many people drove to away games in the Midwest. To drive 400 or 500 miles to be at the game on Saturday was an ordinary pilgrimage for the Oklahoma faithful."

For Butler, who'd grown up devoted to the University of Kentucky, this fanatical attachment to a college team was nothing new. Adolph Rupp instilled this same caliber of loyalty with his basketball success at

Lexington. What was new to Butler was traveling to an away game in such style. From his country-boy point of view, Ed Abbey's T-bird was transportation as exotic as Aladdin's magic carpet. Don't forget, O. J.'s family didn't even own a horse when he was growing up, let alone a car. To Butler, this cruising along in an open-top convertible on a road-trip to see a major college football game, was a trip to last a man a lifetime. The game itself was anticlimactic. As expected, the Sooners crushed the Longhorns on their way to another National Championship. The score was insignificant. The trip was the dream. "The sense of freedom and exhilaration I felt riding in Abbey's open T-bird is a feeling I'll always remember. I'm surprised I never bought a convertible. I always swore I would when I could afford one. Hey, maybe…"

A DREAM DEFERRED

Butler did well his freshman year, in the classroom, on the hardwood floor, and on the baseball diamond. The classroom wasn't as tough as he thought it would be, but maybe it was the discipline of the Air Force that gave him an edge. He didn't have any trouble making himself sit down and study. He kept up with his reading and he had a good memory so school just sort of took care of itself. But in the gym it was tougher.

"There were nine guys my size on scholarship. [The big man was still a rarity in the 1950s.] No longer was I the best shooter, passer, or dribbler like I was in high school." Fortunately, Butler was still the quickest defender. His speed and agility helped to keep him in Grayson's top seven rotation even though he had to bust his butt every day to stay in front of the other eight guys his size battling for playing time.

Besides playing basketball, Butler played baseball his freshman year at Oklahoma, too. Again, he couldn't play varsity because of NCAA rules, but he caught the varsity coach's eye in their practices and scrimmages against the upper-classmen. Butler figured to make the varsity next season in both basketball and baseball. He was poised to become a big man on campus. But destiny has a funny way of pitching people curve balls.

In November of 1954, Butler's sophomore year, his intercollegiate sports career came to a screeching halt when he collapsed on the gym floor after dominating the first half of a preseason scrimmage. He had played the entire half and had hit every outside shot and free-throw he took. He had a number of assists and steals, plus he'd scored 15 points. He knew the coaches were pleased with his play. He was hoping to make the varsity. Then, just as the half ended, down Butler went with a thud to the floor.

Right away the coaches knew it must be serious. O. J. was in the best shape of anyone on the team. He'd been running circles around everyone else, as he always did. During conditioning drills he consistently finished first. If he was unconscious on the floor, something must be critically wrong.

Butler remembered, "When I came to, my heart was racing in a wild irregular manner. It felt like it wanted to pound right through my chest. I was woozy, light-headed, and everything was spinning, but after laying there a while everything sort of slowed down. When I finally felt good enough to get up, I was taken to the hospital."

By evening O. J. felt like his old normal self, but he was kept overnight for tests and observation. The next afternoon he was released, though with the stipulation that he could not practice until the test results came back. A couple of days later they did and the results were not in Butler's favor. Tests concluded he had tachycardia (an above normal irregular heartbeat, often exacerbated by exercise, which could lead to a heart attack at any time). Butler didn't care, he wanted to resume playing basketball. Drake wanted him to resume playing too, but when the doctors warned the university coaching staff that Butler's life was at risk if he continued to play, there was only one decision Drake could make. The university couldn't afford the risk of liability in light of the doctor's formal diagnosis. For Butler's own good, he was forced to give up his spot on the roster, although he was welcome to continue on as a non-paid assistant if he wanted to remain with the program.

Butler was shattered, but never one to give up without a fight, he thought he could get around this obstacle by transferring to another college where his condition was unknown. In his naïveté he never had a chance. Each school he contacted called Bruce Drake, who unfolded the heart of the mystery behind Butler's desire to transfer.

Butler poignantly recalled, "I was desperate. Playing ball was everything to me. I needed a way through or around this catastrophe. I tried everything I could think of, but the choice was taken out of my hands. My heart broke in five million pieces. I guess I cried for two weeks."

Nonetheless, how does the old saying go? Where one door closes another opens. The playing door closed, but a door Butler never considered before began to creak open. It was a portal to another way of staying in the game—coaching. Hadn't Drake and Grayson suggested that he could help them with practices? Like a lightning-bolt-flash straight from the basketball gods, it hit him. "If I can't play, I'll finish my degree and become a teacher and a coach."

Had destiny dictated any other path, I wouldn't be writing this book.

SUMMER EMPLOYMENT

To get through college Butler needed summer employment when the GI Bill stopped paying (you only got a check while you were enrolled full-time in classes). During his freshman summer he worked in Durant, Oklahoma for the Highways Department for .75 cents an hour. He took a room in a widow woman's house that cost $20 a week for room and board. He was one of six boarders. In his free hours he played baseball in the evenings and on weekends. There was little margin for dating money, which may explain why O. J. only dated one girl, Charlotte Anderson, his entire four years in college.

By the summer of his sophomore year everything had changed. While there was nothing to keep him from playing recreation baseball and basketball in the summer (recreation league officials didn't care if he had a heart attack), there was really no point to it either. He no longer needed to keep his skills sharp by playing ball every day. So O. J. decided to take his sister and brother-in-law up on their offer to come to Chicago and live with them for the summer where he could save up all the money he made working at one of their friend's General Electric Oil filling stations for $1 an hour. Butler hitchhiked to get there.

Butler had a productive summer in Chicago working 10, 12 and 14 hour shifts. He banked nearly all his money. His sister, Emma Lou, was pretty well off. She and her husband were in the convalescent home business. They were also adamant about helping O. J. get through college but they weren't going to just give him money. They helped out by providing him with free room and board, and getting him a summer job where he could put in a lot of hours, allowing him to save nearly $1200 that summer. To thank them, he wanted to take them to a baseball game at the end of the summer, but they wouldn't hear of it. They didn't want him wasting his money, and besides, they weren't sports fans.

Baseball was Butler's only vice that summer. Whenever he could work it out, he'd buy a cheap ticket for a dollar in the Wrigley Field bleacher bums' section of the outfield, and enjoy an afternoon game; and yeah, you guessed it, he brought his mitt along in the grip he hitchhiked with to Chicago. The big game he wanted to take his sister and brother-in-law to was a game between the Cubs and the Dodgers in late August. After his sister and brother-in-law turned down his offer he bought himself a ticket in June to make sure he'd get in. He looked forward all summer to that game which would take place just prior to his returning to Oklahoma to begin his junior year.

"As a fanatical baseball fan," Butler smilingly remembered, "I always loved the Dodgers. They were the first major league team to give a 'colored' man [the politically correct term at the time for someone of African descent] the opportunity to compete outside of the Negro leagues. Way back in 1947, when I was a sophomore in high school, Jackie Robinson became my hero, and I loved the Dodgers for giving him the chance."

Now you might wonder how a boy from Tennessee, growing up in St. Louis Cardinal territory, could become a Dodger fan? All his friends hated the Dodgers, especially when they added Jackie Robinson to the team. As a poor white man's son in Bemis, Butler was expected to look down on coloreds like his friends did. They had that poor white-trash mentality that believed, if you aren't better than a black man, who are you better than? But unlike his friends, O. J. never developed the ubiquitous Southern racist mentality. Sure, he'd grown up with segregation in the schools and neighborhoods. He knew the code of the South: coloreds had to be off the streets by sundown or risk mayhem. Yet, for some atypical reason, O. J. never developed one prejudiced bone in his entire body.

Perhaps it was because his family did the same menial labor many poor negroes were relegated to. Growing up under the same hardships and privations that poverty imposed on Southern blacks, Butler commiserated with their hard times. Other factors that influenced his unprejudiced views were that his parents never used racial epithets nor did they discuss matters of race. The worst pressure for Butler in regard to racism and discrimination came from school. "Behind my back," Butler said, "but not too far behind it, my St. Louis Cardinal fan friends would sometimes call me a 'n—lover' (Butler refuses to say the word even when quoting others). And for some reason that I can't consciously explain, all that did was make me feel an even stronger affinity for them."

Throughout the dog-days of summer, Butler looked forward to the Cubs / Dodgers game like a kid anticipating Christmas in November. "Seeing Jackie Robinson play," Butler recalled, "was a reward that motivated me whenever I got a little moody over the fact that all I ever did was work and sleep." As the summer drew to a close, O. J. got more excited. He'd never seen his beloved Dodgers play. He'd heard them on the radio and read about them in the papers, but he'd missed the few new-fangled television broadcasts he might have caught if he'd been in the right places at the right times. So this game was going to be a big deal.

Finally, the day of the game arrived. By now Butler owned a car—a 1946 Ford with a grabby clutch, purchased for $75, very dependable once you got it out of first gear but nothing stylish. After working his final shift of the summer, O. J. knocked off early in order to drive out to his sister's north-side house to clean up and change for the game. He thanked his boss for the summer employment, pocketed his pay and hit the road shortly before noon. As he drove he noticed thunderclouds gathering in the distance over Lake Michigan—not an uncommon sight in late August, but by the time he got to his sister's house the clouds looked ominous.

O. J. bathed, then ate the last home-cooked meal he would get until Thanksgiving. The next morning he was leaving for Oklahoma. Around 1:00 p.m. he piled back into the Ford, gunned the motor, and wheeled onto the expressway just ahead of the clouds. Before he got halfway to the stadium however, the first raindrop hit his windshield and by the time he reached Wrigley Field 10 minutes later the rain had increased into a deluge of Noah's Ark proportions.

Undeterred, O. J. opened an umbrella and stomped through the accumulating puddles to the gate with all the other optimistic fans. He kept his eyes down, not wanting to acknowledge what looked like official notice of the game's postponement being affixed to the ticket booth window as he approached the turnstyle.

"Hold on!" Butler insisted. "Maybe the rain will stop."

The ticket-taker chuckled. "A front has just moved in from Canada and the forecast is 100% for rain for the next couple of hours." Already the puddle O. J. was standing in had deepened to about half an inch. The ticket-taker added, "And even if the rain does stop soon, the field will be too wet to play on. No problem, your ticket is still good. They'll play a double-header the day after tomorrow to make the game up. Just bring your ticket back then."

Butler turned around dejected. He shuffled back to his car muttering, then drove to his sister's house in silence. He had to leave for Oklahoma tomorrow, he couldn't put off the drive two days or he'd miss signing up for his fall classes. Registration was on a first-come first-serve basis. He would not be able to use his rain-check ticket. He gave the ticket to his brother-in-law to give to one of his friends.

As it turned out, Butler never got to see his hero Jackie Robinson play in person, though he did eventually get to see him play on TV. Robinson retired before Butler was able to see the Dodgers in person after they moved to California. However, as a measure of compensation, Butler did get to see Sandy Koufax pitch a perfect game for the Dodgers against the Cubs on September 8, 1965. Koufax retired 27 consecutive Cubs to earn his fourth career no-hitter. Still, as historical a game as that was, it wasn't the same as seeing his hero Jackie Robinson. Butler flashed back to the rained out game at Wrigley in 1955 and snickered. He still hates Chicago weather.

Back at school for his junior year, Butler did better than ever academically, although he did suffer one setback. He decided to coach a local high school basketball team and that took time away from his studies, time he dearly needed for one particular class: physiology. Butler acknowledges physiology would have been tough even if he had put in the necessary study time, but without the extra effort he was courting disaster. In the end, he bombed the final and failed physiology by one percentage point; however, he thought he could talk his teacher into giving him that one percent. "I went in and tried talking Dr. Harvey into changing my grade, but she was too tough a nut to crack, Southern charm and all."

She told me, "Butler, you failed! It doesn't matter that it was only by one percent. You have to repeat MY CLASS next term, and you will pass it with no less than a C. That's all there is to it."

"Well, that's just what happened," Butler said, "and from her I learned a valuable lesson I never forgot in all my years of teaching and coaching: a point here and a point there always add up, and ultimately they make the difference between success and failure, between winning and losing." The rest of Butler's classes were a breeze compared to Dr. Harvey's physiology class, and by the end of May, 1956, Butler had completed his junior year coursework on schedule.

Butler now only needed one more summer job to see him through his senior year, but he didn't really want go back to Chicago and work at the filling station again. That had been too much work and not enough fun. When he graduated the following year, it would be work, work, work, for the next 35 years. *Why not try and have a little fun this summer? Surely there are some jobs I can make money at without having to bust my tail for three months in the summer heat.*

Hoping to find something that paid well but wasn't too much of a grind, Butler jumped at his buddy Rick Roland's suggestion that they take an offer to drive a brand new car to California. Roland, a varsity swimmer, was well connected. His dad had a friend who was a big-shot Cadillac dealer who needed to have a special edition green Cadillac delivered from Kansas City to Monterey, CA. in two days. The pay was $100 each, plus travel expenses. There might even be a summer job at the Monterey dealership once they got there. Butler, who had never been to California, nor had ever driven a Cadillac, jumped at this fling at adventure.

Once in Monterey, it turned out there was no need for two lot-boys at the Cadillac dealership. Since Roland had gotten them the job driving the cars out, Butler figured he owed it to Rick to let him have the summer lot-boy job. But what would he do in Monterey? He spent a couple of days futilely looking for work, but after being turned down by every one he talked to O. J. was discouraged. Besides being unemployed and a long ways from anything familiar, he also quickly found out he was not a fan of the damp, cool, often overcast coastline climate. At the Monterey Employment

Development Office he was told there was plenty of work in Southern California. With his $100 earnings dissipating daily, he decided he'd try his luck down Los Angeles way.

Uneventfully, O. J. hitchhiked down the Pacific Coast Highway in one day. That night he took a room at the Los Angeles YMCA, then went by bus to the Los Angeles Employment Development Office the next morning. As destiny would have it, Butler was directed to a new amusement park that was hiring in Anaheim. "The Happiest Place on Earth," Disneyland, a one-year-old 160 acre theme park, was seeking college students and teachers to fill their summer ranks. Disneyland had only been open on a part-time basis the first year but this summer they were opening full-time. With an expectation of two million summer visitors, Disneyland desperately needed to fill hundreds of jobs with enthusiastic, bright-eyed, idealistic, college-educated employees who would project their "pursuit of happiness" image.

Disneyland looked exactly like what Butler had hoped for in summer employment—a good time while getting paid. "I was no stranger to manual labor," Butler reflected. "Loading kids onto Dumbo the Flying Elephant didn't sound all that tough. After working at a gas station and for the Highway Department the two previous summers, this sounded more like a vacation than work; besides, at $3.15 an hour, I'd be making $25 a day, that was close to what I made in a week working for the Oklahoma Highway Department."

Butler was hired immediately. As he recalls it, "I had the distinction of being the first out-of-state college student hired by Disneyland." An hour after interviewing, Butler was in uniform and reporting to his first assignment. Owing to the fact that he still retained his Tennessee twang, he was put at the helm of the Mark Twain steamship. And like Mark Twain, who piloted riverboats from New Orleans to St. Louis, this was the best job that Butler had ever had.

During his first two weeks at Disneyland, O. J. faithfully steered the cable-guided paddleboat around Tom Sawyer's Island, regaling cosmopolitan visitors with a scripted monologue—that he never failed to embellish on. Then, when the rafts opened at the end of his first two weeks, O. J., with his Southern accent, fair skin, and freckle-faced complexion, was promoted to a Tom Sawyer look-a-like position as head raftsman ferrying guests to Tom Sawyer's Island from the mainland. His bosses loved him already. He was a natural in this line of work.

Butler liked the improvisation he could use in the character of Tom Sawyer. He quickly memorized his script, but prided himself on throwing in his own twists and amateur theatrics. "Every Sunday at 3:00 p.m. I gave the visitors a tall tale about the island and the secret cave filled with treasure. Just as I was getting to the part about where the treasure was hidden, I would lose my balance and fall off the raft backward and flail about in the water as if I were drowning. Then, I would stand up and shock everyone. The water was only three feet deep. The guests loved it."

Butler worked at Disneyland for six consecutive summers, and in those six summers, Disneyland was very good to Butler. That's where he met his future wife. "There was a back lot where employees took their breaks. One afternoon I laid eyes on the prettiest girl I ever saw. She was smoking a cigarette so I walked over to her and said, 'You know, cigarettes are bad for your health.'" That was Butler's big come-on line. Wow! If I weren't married I'd try that one myself. NOT! But the surprising thing about it is, it worked. Her name was Sharon LaBonte.

O. J. TAKES A NEW NAME

In September of 1956, within the first week of returning for his senior year at Oklahoma, O. J. got a heart-wrenching call from his mother. Oliver Jackson Butler, O. J.'s hard-working, unassuming father had passed away from a heart attack. (O. J.'s own tachycardia flared up a little at the news.) "Right away, about five different friends offered me the keys to their cars," Butler remembered. He took one up on his offer and drove straight home to again help with the funeral arrangements and spend a week with his family. Naturally, he had no idea how great an effect this week would have on him—so much so that he would return to college with a new name.

Going through his father's account books after his death, it was discovered the family's financial foundation was still in a precarious position. Oliver Jackson had gotten out of sharecropping when Ollie was beginning secondary school. He found work in the grocery store business. Then, about the time Ollie had joined the Air Force, his father turned entrepreneurial. He'd been able to take over a little country store and the family's pecuniary difficulties had eased up for the first time ever. But, as we know from Shakespeare's *Hamlet*, what "seems" and what "is" are almost never the same. The store was actually heavily in debt. Even with Carl Perkins, the country-western song writer and singer (of "Blue Suede Shoes" fame) sitting on the porch of that store in Tennessee, strumming his guitar and entertaining the customers before he'd risen to pop culture icon status, Oliver Jackson was unable to make the money he'd hoped the store would yield. Fortunately, O. J.'s sister Emma Lou came to the rescue. She and her husband settled the store's accounts, making good on the debts their father's dream couldn't pay off.

When O. J. returned to college, he knew he'd have to work hard to catch up on what he had missed. To give him added motivation, he came back as a new man, literally. He'd gotten it into his head that he wanted to honor his father's memory by dropping the initials his parents had christened him with and begin using his father's name, Oliver Jackson. His friends at school found Oliver a little too stiff, but "Ollie" they liked. From then on, Butler became "Ollie" to his friends, and that's the way I'll refer to him now for the rest of this book, although it's always been a little difficult for me to call him by his first name after so many years of calling him "Mr. Butler" or "Coach."

Ollie's senior year passed quickly. He coached the same local high school team again for a second season. (I'll tell you more about that in the next chapter.) He also continued to help out occasionally with the Oklahoma University basketball program as a volunteer whenever he had some free hours, something he'd continued to do since leaving the team as a player. He had a strenuous load of classes to attend to. But all in all his life was running smoothly—firing on all cylinders you might say.

In June of 1957, a monumental achievement carried Ollie Butler to new heights. Graduation day! His mother and sister took the train out to Oklahoma to witness this glorious accomplishment. The son of a second grade dropout and a poor sharecropper father, Ollie was the first member of his family to earn a college degree.

Was that really him on the dais shaking hands with the university president? If only his father were here. His mother and sister beamed blissfully as the tassel on his graduation cap was ceremoniously shifted from one side to the other. They were so proud. First the Air Force and now college. He had a summer job at Disneyland in the golden land of California, and a full-time teaching job lined up for September. Despite the hardships of his upbringing, Ollie kept transcending. Long ago he had set his mind on making something of himself. Step by step he had moved onward in that pursuit. Mother and sister both sat musing: *How far up would he rise?*

ST. JOSEPH'S

When Butler's playing days at Oklahoma came to an end during his sophomore year in college, and he determined he would become a coach as well as a teacher, he continued on with the Oklahoma University basketball program as a volunteer assistant through the 1954-55 season to learn as much as he could. At the end of the season the Bruce Drake era ended. He retired after coaching at OU since 1929. Butler wasn't sure if the new coach would want or need his help the following season so he started looking around for a high school team in the vicinity of the university that he could coach himself. In the fall of 1956, St. Joseph's Catholic School in Norman, Oklahoma, offered him a job. (Perhaps it was an omen that the St. Joseph Knights' school colors were green and white, the same as the Victor Valley Jackrabbits where Butler would eventually end up for 32 years.) The pay was minimal, but Butler wasn't in it for the extra money. What he wanted was experience.

Butler coached there two years. The first year his team went 15-10. The second year they were 12-10. Butler used a lot of what he had learned at Oklahoma in his St. Joe's practices. He also experimented with some new ideas he creatively improvised to compliment the team's limited talent. When he left in 1957, St. Joe's did everything they could to keep Butler except give him the one thing he needed, a salary comparable to what first year public high school teachers were making. They wanted to but couldn't afford it and Butler felt bad because he wanted to stay at St. Joe's.

Butler's initial coaching experience there was so enjoyable that he didn't have a doubt that he wanted to teach and coach for an entire career. For one thing, it allowed him to continue playing. He loved competing with the boys in practice, just not at a level where his heart condition would flare up. He'd play in three on three games, run the half-court offense with the boys and engage in shooting competitions. This is what drove him, the competitive spirit. He just had to keep himself from getting too carried away and wanting to run full-court.

"St. Joe's was a small K-12 school," Butler said. "It was a great place for me to start. There weren't more than 50 boys and girls total in the whole high school. Right away I realized I had to learn how to teach technique since there wasn't much of a talent pool to choose from." It was also in those first two years at St. Joe's that Butler learned primary lessons about winning, the first being that in order to win consistently you have to have talent. A good coach can only teach so much. Without talent to go along with the skills players have been taught, a team won't win regularly no matter how good the coaching.

In comparison to the public schools they played, St. Joe's was about ten times smaller in student enrollment and even the Catholic schools they played in the diocese were quite a bit bigger, too. But Butler quickly established himself as a coach who made a difference in neutralizing a school's size. St. Joe's would go into Oklahoma City and Tulsa for tournaments and compete with those bigger schools. They didn't always win but rarely did they get blown out. They stayed in the game because Butler taught his smaller, slower, and less talented players how to utilize their strengths and compensate for their weaknesses with proper technique.

Butler remembered his first season at St. Joe's. "Every boy who tried out for the team made it, but only two of them were any good—Red Miser and Jimmy Dickerson." To show you what an impact Butler made on those boys, nearly 50 years later Butler and Dickerson are still close friends. Miser has since passed away.

Dickerson was a fatherless boy attending St. Joseph's for its discipline and guidance. Butler, 25 years old at the time, wasn't that much older than the boys on his team. He became a big brother figure to many of them, especially Dickerson. They grew close in the two years Butler was there though after Dickerson graduated and joined the military they lost track of each other for a number of years.

Butler told me about their friendship with a certain uncharacteristic sentimentality that struck me as a bit off kilter. Ollie Butler is not the sentimental type. When he coached us in the 1970s he was TOUGH! He wasn't our buddy or a big brother type, neither was he a paternal figure. He was our coach, the man in charge, a demigod. When he was talking we kept our mouths shut. He was the kind of coach who said what he meant and meant what he said, and if he said "Jump!" you know what our response was. If he told us to run until we hit the wall, we did. It was his way or the highway but he earned our respect every step of the way by being fair, practical, competent, believable, and an imperious leader we never doubted. But this Dickerson thing? How could he have been so different with those boys at St. Joe's? Well, for one thing, he was in his mid-forties when he coached us and not a novice in his mid-twenties like he was back then. In 1975 he was 30 years older than us, not seven or eight years older than the boys he coached at St. Joe's. I'm sure that accounts for why he was a lot closer to those boys than he was to us.

In 1994, when Butler was roasted at a retirement party at the Holiday Inn in Victorville, CA, Jimmy Dickerson flew in from Oklahoma. He was the only player to represent any of the teams Butler coached in the 1950s.

Why did he go to all that expense to attend a retirement party for a guy he hadn't seen since 1957? I called him to find out.

"Ollie Butler had a tremendous influence on me," Dickerson said. "He helped me grow up. He showed me how hard work and dedication can pay off. He was the best coach I ever had."

Dickerson recalled several anecdotes about his St. Joe's days on the basketball team. I prefer the one about Butler taking him and some of the other guys on the team to watch college tournaments in Oklahoma City. To me this story typifies Butler's commitment to the game and to the young men it involved. So, in the spirit of brevity, I will only mention it and apologize for leaving out some of Dickerson's other colorful memories: "We saw some of the biggest stars in college basketball at tournaments in Oklahoma City. [Mr. Dickerson didn't mention any specific names, but Butler said they saw Wilt Chamberlain.] Coach would explain everything the teams were doing. He explained about the defenses and offenses. He knew things about the game that we had never even heard of. He had an absolutely brilliant basketball mind. We were all in awe of him."

Dickerson said Butler's love for basketball was so passionate that it rubbed off on them. Butler instilled an earnestness for the game in them while also inspiring their admiration and respect. "Coach wasn't that much older than us players," Dickerson added, "so he treated us like equals. We were amazed at how naturally he related to us. Here was a guy who'd moved halfway across the country from his home state, he'd already done a tour of duty in the Air Force, and he was a student at the university who was spending his free time coaching us. He seemed to know something about everything, yet he treated us like we were his friends."

Dickerson felt Butler's key to success as a coach was his gift for teaching. He said that the fundamentals Butler taught in the gym were so well explained that he was able to apply the principles he learned as a teenager to his softball and golf games as an adult.

"There aren't enough Ollie Butlers in the world," Dickerson closed our interview with. "We need more dedicated caring people like him. I was a kid without a dad, and he came into my life at just the right time. I can't tell you how glad I am I got to know him!"

When I hung up the phone at the conclusion of our interview, I was overcome with a sense of WOW! Here was Jimmy Dickerson, a man in his sixties who had been powerfully impacted by Ollie Butler a half century back, yet the impression Butler made all those years ago reverberated through him like the events had just taken place yesterday. Truly, a good coach can make a powerful difference in a kid's life.

Butler was extremely busy during the two years he coached at St. Joe's. When Bruce Drake retired at Oklahoma in 1955, his successor, Doyle

Parrick, it turned out, was happy to have Butler continue on as a volunteer assistant with the program. During basketball season Butler spent countless hours each afternoon soaking up college basketball drills and skills at Owens Fieldhouse, the University of Oklahoma's gym, before passing what he'd learned on to his boys at St. Joseph's. And that's how he learned to coach. Butler also made some good connections at this time. It was Doyle Parrick's phone call to a school superintendent in nearby Noble that would get Butler his first salaried teaching job and his affiliation with Oklahoma freshman coach John Grayson would also pay off down the employment road ahead.

Butler caught the coaching bug bad while working with the boys at St. Joe's. An overwhelming sense of purpose and satisfaction enveloped him. He knew this was what he was meant to do. He also realized that if he was to do it well, he needed to focus on what end results he wanted to achieve. As Stephen R. Covey says in his book, *The 7 Habits of Highly Effective People*, "Begin with the end in mind." Butler was ahead of his time, he realized this long before Covey started putting on his motivational seminars.

Beginning with the end in mind is all about knowing where you want to go, so at the outset of his career Butler began thinking about what he wanted to accomplish as a coach. By the end of his second year at St. Joe's he knew and set his first three long-term goals: the first goal was to win at least 500 games as a head coach; the second goal was to finish with a winning percentage of no lower than 70%; and his third goal was to keep a single varsity program going for 25 consecutive years. As you will see, he achieved all three. Furthermore, besides setting long-term goals, Butler determined to get serious about the immediate.

In the fall of 1956, while in the midst of taking a full-load of classes during his senior year at Oklahoma, Butler also created a self-directed course in the science of basketball. He read every book on basketball available at the time in the Oklahoma University library. First, he wanted to do the best job he could to prepare himself for his second season at St. Joe's; and, second, he would soon be entering the competitive job market upon graduating from college and wanted every edge he could get to help him secure his first full-time teaching and coaching job.

This academic approach to the game would continue throughout Butler's career. Even after he landed at his final destination, Victor Valley High School, he continued to read books on basketball, attend clinics, observe college practices, work at camps, and analyze the games he watched on TV, whether college or professional.

Butler listened to everyone and appropriated whatever would work for his program. He was never too proud to borrow good strategies and effective drills. After going to a clinic or reading a new book by a famous coach, Butler would implement sound strategies he'd learned. Maybe he'd reposition his players in the full-court press by switching from a 1-2-2 to a 2-1-2 or a 2-2-1 alignment. Perhaps he'd modify a man-to-man defense into a match-up zone defense or put a new wrinkle in his offensive passing game. Yet, with whatever innovations he thought might help his current squad compete better, his core game goals remained constant: hold the opponent under 50 points, out-rebound them, and convert 50% of their turnovers into points.

Even in retirement Butler is still learning. Recently he visited John Wooden at a Pasadena Bookstore, the way he has done every time Wooden brings out a new book. He bought a copy of *Be Quick, But Don't Hurry* and had Wooden autograph it. After a few nostalgic words with his aging mentor, Butler headed for home anxious to get through the rush hour traffic so he could sit down and read Wooden's latest thoughts on the game.

As a premier student of the game, Butler, like Wooden, would later become known as a sage consultant in high school coaching circles. In the twilight of his career and in retirement he was (and actually still is) regularly contacted by coaches just getting started in the game. (That's how I got the earliest inklings of inspiration for this book—in case you skimmed over the introduction.) I contacted Butler myself about some strategy when I took over the freshman team at VVHS in the mid 1990s under Kurt Herbst, Butler's successor. I'll never forget a key bit of advice Butler gave me back then: "Never try to do something in a game that you haven't already worked on in practice, it won't work!" But of course I forgot his advice, and when I tried something new that we hadn't ever practiced in a close game with a 16-0 freshman team in 1999, we quickly became a 16-1 team. Later, I remembered Butler's words, "It won't work," as I dejectedly rode home on the bus justly blaming myself for ruining our perfect record with bad coaching strategy.

GETTING PAID TO DO WHAT YOU LOVE

In September of 1957, following college graduation and a second summer working at Disneyland, Butler began his first paid teaching job at Noble High School in Noble, Oklahoma—courtesy of Doyle Parrick's connection with the local superintendent, John Hubbard. The old saying is true for a reason. It's not what you know it's who you know.

At Noble, Butler was hired to teach history and driver's education for $2700 a year—though before the year started everyone got a $300 raise. He was also to coach the 7th, 8th, 9th, 10th and varsity basketball and baseball teams for an additional $800—which made it easier for Butler to afford his steep rent of $40 a month.

Not long into the basketball season, Butler figured out why the superintendent had been so anxious to hire him. He had two boys on the team, one was a 10th grader and the other a senior. The senior, John Hubbard Jr., started on the varsity and was a good player for Butler. His younger brother, however, would panic under pressure, so he didn't get too many minutes in games. Because of this, in Butler's opinion, the superintendent turned out to be a "horse's ass." He wanted Butler to give his younger son more playing time and figured Butler owed him a favor since he had gotten him the job.

"The superintendent's younger son (Butler doesn't remember the boy's name) was a good kid. He never complained. He worked hard, and he wasn't a "pain in the ass" like his dad," said Butler, "but I couldn't see him helping the team in games. He was strictly a practice player who would get into games only if we were winning or losing by a lot of points." The kid knew his place though and was happy just to be a member of the team. Butler wished his whiny father could accept that too. However, like a lot of battles we fight in life, this conflict turned out to be a blessing in disguise for young coach Butler. It taught him a valuable lesson about coach-parent relations.

The superintendent, through some distortion of reality, thought his younger son was an Olympic caliber athlete. Butler saw it differently. The boy was thrilled to get into a blowout game for a couple of minutes at the end; he never displayed a brooding attitude about spending the majority of his time on the bench—but his dad, what a case! Following every game the superintendent chipped away at Butler regarding his younger boy's lack of playing time.

Finally, after one particularly annoying ear-chewing, Butler turned on the superintendent and asked him, "Is my job to win games or to play everyone?"

"Well, to win games, of course," replied the superintendent.

"Then leave me alone to play the players I think will help us win," Butler replied. "If at the end of the season you don't like the results, you can fire me. Your boy is a great kid but right now he can't help us win."

Direct and to the point. Cut and dried. The superintendent never wheedled Butler again. And Butler made a mental note at Noble that year, *Never let outside influences dictate who you play and who you don't. Play the players who will help you win.* In retrospect, Butler had to admit, "I may not have figured that out so early in my career had it not been for that situation."

This was Butler's third season as a head coach and his career was picking up steam. After going 27-20 in his first two years at St Joseph's, his team at Noble went 23-6 and won the District Championship for the first time in the school's history, defeating the previous year's State Champs, Purcell, on their own court. Butler, who has a photographic memory for every basketball game he ever played in or coached, replayed the final scene of that game: "With 12 seconds left John Hubbard Jr. tipped the ball to Jim Southard who faked to drive then pulled up and let go a 20 foot jumper from the corner that swished through the net to break a 58-58 tie as the buzzer sounded. After the game, Bony Matthews, Purcell's coach, tried to shake my hand but couldn't. The fans had rushed the floor and hoisted me up on their shoulders and paraded me around the gym like some conquering war hero and I have to admit it was better than any congratulatory handshake. Unfortunately, we lost our next game in the Regionals."

At Noble, Butler also learned a little lesson about giving players rides home after practice. When the varsity baseball tryouts began, Butler found out he had a great pitcher, an Indian named Jim Little Jim. Little Jim told Butler the first day that he could play only if someone could give him a ride home each day. Without asking for particulars, Butler volunteered. Surprise! That evening Butler discovered Jim Little Jim lived 25 miles from the school, giving him a 50 mile round trip each night after both practices and games. Though Butler continued to give rides to players throughout his coaching career, from that point on he made it a practice to ask in advance where his players lived, just so he wouldn't be blind-sided by an extra hour of driving after a three hour practice.

ROMANCE

In June of 1958, after a highly successful year teaching and coaching at Noble, Butler resigned and returned to his summer job at Disneyland for the third year in a row. He wanted to find a teaching and coaching job in California. It turned out to be fortuitous that he left Noble behind. This was the year he met Sharon LaBonte. She was a ticket clerk in a Hawaiian village Adventure Land shop and a full-time college student who had recently moved from San Bernardino to nearby Santa Ana. He was 28. She was going on 20. You remember his opening line.

When I asked about their first date, Sharon acted like I should be able to guess, the answer being so obvious. "He took me to a Dodger game," she said with a wry smile. "I brought along my sewing."

Sharon wasn't much of a sports enthusiast but as with the boys at St. Joe's and Noble, Ollie's love for sports was infectious; by the end of the game Sharon was holding Ollie's hand and cheering right along with him, she'd put her sewing away in the third inning. A month of dating later, Butler was smitten and knew he wanted to marry Sharon. He began looking earnestly for a full-time teaching and coaching job near Santa Ana.

Butler applied throughout the greater Los Angeles area and in mid-August, miraculously it seemed, just as he was about to give up hope and begin packing for Oklahoma, Dominguez High School called him in for an interview. They had an opening for a driver's education teacher and needed a varsity basketball coach. *Perfect*! thought Butler. He interviewed and felt it went well. It must have. The next day they called and offered him the job. His future was set. Now he'd be able to stay in California and marry Sharon.

Until disaster struck at the very end of August, Butler was on Cloud Nine.

Ten days before school was to begin, Dominguez High called Butler back and gave him bad news. Butler's California Teaching Credential in Driver's Ed. would not be cleared in time for school's opening. The paperwork from Oklahoma was lost in transit. To start the process over would take as long as a month. (At that time it was the law in California that schools must begin the year with fully credentialed teachers. There was no such thing as emergency credentialing then like there is today.) Thunderstruck, Butler was out of a job.

Scrambling the whole week prior to Labor Day weekend, Butler took as many breaks as he could from his Disneyland raftsman job. He spent his breaks on the phone calling every junior high and high school in a fifty mile radius. Unfortunately, there wasn't any teacher shortage then like there is today. Every position was filled. "Each day closer to the end of summer made me feel more desperate," Butler lamented. "My summer job at Disneyland concluded on Labor Day. Normally I'd be back at school two days later. I didn't know what I'd do if I didn't get something before then."

IDAHO STATE

Like a desperate passenger grasping at floating wreckage after washing overboard from a sinking ship, Butler grabbed for anything that would keep him afloat as a coach and teacher. Fortunately, just before he was about to go down, his former college freshman coach, John Grayson, now the head basketball coach at Idaho State in Pocatello, threw him a lifeline. Grayson used his influence to get Butler hired on as a graduate assistant on his own coaching staff. All Butler had to do was enroll in master's degree courses. Done!

Butler didn't relish leaving Sharon but it couldn't be helped. Their romance was flourishing and he hoped to marry her once he settled in at Dominguez High. This change of plan was a definite setback to marriage. He let Sharon know he was going to Idaho State grudgingly but with the hope that this interim job would work into something permanent so they could get married the following year. Neither Sharon nor Ollie would confess the promises they made as he prepared to drive north.

The day after Labor Day, Butler packed up the Pontiac he had most recently acquired, and after one last picnic with Sharon he drove straight through to Pocatello in about 15 hours. Grayson got him into a dorm. The next day Butler enrolled in a secondary education program that would earn him his MA in education. As a graduate assistant he would earn $50 a month and the college would pay for his books, tuition, room, and meals (Monday through Friday in the cafeteria).

Butler knew he would have to be resourceful in supplementing his meager $50 a month income. After expenses each month he only had about $12 remaining. One money-saving scheme he thought up was a food co-op. He and his roommate bought a bushel of apples to eat on the weekend when the college cafeteria was closed. They had apples for breakfast, lunch and dinner. This saved them at least a couple of bucks each per weekend. They ate them every way imaginable: sliced, whole, halved, quartered, diced, and well, you name it and they tried it. They even thought about making and selling some hard cider from the overripe apples.

A more lucrative monetary supplement was a low-stakes gambling conspiracy. Butler and Roy Griffen, one of the Idaho State players, teamed up in a little petty larceny plot. Each Saturday night when some of the stars on the team got together to play penny-ante poker, Butler and Griffen would exchange cards under the table. They were only after enough money to afford a movie on Sunday afternoon. They would work the table until they had made enough to afford their movie tickets, a coke each, and a bag of popcorn, then they would each casually drop out of the game. They knew it was devious, yet taking advantage of rubes has a long tradition in America, and for such low stakes their consciences didn't bother them too bad. Besides, did you ever try to eat apples at a matinee?

Butler loved his education courses. To him they were easy. He wrote an outstanding research paper on the role of the coach as a guidance counselor that earned him special recognition from a couple of professors, they even urged him to publish it in a professional journal. (I have a copy if you'd like to see it.) But it was the coaching opportunity that Butler relished more than anything. He was at a Division I NCAA college, working under an up and coming coach who wanted to take the program to heights never before achieved. Next to being with Sharon, this was heaven. He was soaking up more basketball knowledge than ever before.

The Idaho State basketball program immediately vaulted to prominence under Grayson. Prior to his arrival they'd been the league's oft beaten step-sister. Grayson had turned them into contenders in the years since he left Drake's program at Oklahoma University. Grayson was a master strategist at putting together a winning game plan that would exploit an opponent's tendencies.

One thing Butler didn't care too much for though was Grayson's penchant for playing favorites. According to Butler, "The stars of the team could do no wrong, and the backup players couldn't do anything right—they were the whipping boys of the team." (Perhaps this explains why Butler didn't mind card-sharking some of those star players out of their loose change.) While Butler took away many good things he learned about basketball from Grayson when he moved on to coach another high school boy's program the following year, he tried to leave behind Grayson's bad habits, which a *Saturday Evening Post* article said included: bad sportsmanship, referee bullying, inciting fans to violence and rowdyism, and using obscenities.

Butler was mostly successful in this. When he coached us he didn't play favorites. There was one set of rules for all, which were pretty easy to know and follow since there were only three: come on time, dress appropriately and work hard. Butler did not pepper his speech with vulgarities or obscenities the way a lot of coaches do and he never tried to whip up the fans to do violence with his courtside behavior, although I can't say his antics didn't sometimes incite the crowd to raucousness. He wasn't a violent person either, though I hear that when he was a younger coach he was known to kick a chair or two. (Steve Scoggin, whom you will meet later, tells of a legendary chair incident. It seemed that after a loss Butler was so mad that he kicked a folding chair in the locker room. The players watched as the chair folded up and flew through the air into the wall where it bounced off, unfolded, and landed upright back where it started. They were amazed and wanted to laugh but didn't dare. Butler, was amazed too. To make his point he walked over to it and kicked it again. The second time it tipped over. He looked at his team with a satisfied smile. All of them burst out laughing.) However, there is one trait of Grayson's Butler may have not been wholly able to exorcise—the referee bullying. Grayson had an inherent distaste for lousy officials and so did Butler. But hey, nobody's perfect.

During Christmas break in 1958, which didn't last very long if you were an assistant basketball coach for Grayson—and low man on the totem pole to boot—Butler managed a quick three day turnaround trip to Santa Ana to visit Sharon and stir up the embers. She was still waiting for him, due mainly to the fact that he'd turned into a pretty good letter writer. (No, she won't let us see any of them.) He promised her that when the school year ended he'd be back for a fourth summer at Disneyland and that one way or another he'd get a job that he could afford to marry her on before summer ended. Ever the optimist, he knew he'd find a teaching and coaching job somewhere, one that wouldn't fall through at the last minute like last summer.

When Butler returned to Pocatello after Christmas, his first assignment was scouting the tournament teams they had coming up on their schedule. Butler earned quite a crafty reputation from this endeavor. The facility hosting the tournament had a game gym and a practice gym. The gym where the tournament teams practiced was two stories high. Butler's assignment was to watch the games between teams they might face in the tournament second and third rounds and prepare a scouting report; but Butler did not confine himself to just watching the tournament games, he also staked out those teams' practices. He made his way to the second floor of the practice gym and spied through a grate in the floor. He diagrammed all their secret plays and when it was Idaho State's turn to practice he showed them to Grayson who then designed the defenses to stop the plays. After all, everyone knows all's fair in love and basketball.

With Butler's leave-no-stone-unturned assistance, Idaho State finished as league champions in a tight conference race in 1958-59, which got them all the way to the second round of the Regionals in the NCAA post-season tournament for the first time in forever. Butler was given quite a bit of credit for helping Grayson engineer their first round win. He had flown out to New Mexico to scout them the previous weekend and done a detailed job of sketching their offensive plays and defensive alignments. He'd analyzed their personnel and created a man by man match-up he thought Grayson could use based on each player's size, quickness, strengths and weaknesses.

He'd even done interviews with local program supporters to find out what New Mexico players were on hot streaks or peaking, feigning all the time to be a reporter. The information was like gold to Grayson and later he said Butler's scouting report was the reason they won that first round game. But what Butler remembers more than Grayson's praise was the pat on the back he earned from the athletic director.

Butler was given $100 expense money for the scouting trip to New Mexico. When he returned the following Monday, he gave the athletic director $50 change, saying he hadn't needed it. "He couldn't believe it," Butler laughed. "After our first round win in the Regionals, he took me out for a steak dinner at the swankest steakhouse in town and he paid for everything as a way of showing his appreciation for me looking out for the school's athletic budget. No one had ever returned expense money before!"

Besides assisting Grayson with the varsity, Butler also coached the Idaho State freshman team to a 5-0 record against some of the other colleges that had freshman teams. When basketball season ended, Grayson asked Butler to return for another year. He saw that Butler had the traits to become a major college basketball coach. Butler, on the other hand, besides being anxious to find a full-time teaching and coaching job that would enable him to marry, saw that coaching at the NCAA level was an all-consuming affair that wouldn't leave time for much of anything else. While he loved the competitiveness of this level of basketball, he realized that high school basketball was where he'd find his niche. It wouldn't involve the year-round headaches of recruiting, dealing with big egos, in-depth scouting and having to win at all costs. He'd learned in one year at Idaho State that basketball wasn't near as much fun when it became a full-time job.

Sharon was on his mind more than ever as the end of the school year approached. He was tired of settling for her sweet scented letters, he yearned for the warmth of her physical presence. He wanted to get married more than anything and a $50 a month graduate assistant coach's pay wasn't going to cut it. He would be turning 29 this year. Sharon was now 20. He wondered how long would she wait for him if he dawdled getting established?

Surprisingly, around mid-April, not long after basketball season ended, Butler started getting unsolicited head coaching offers from Idaho high school districts. Grayson was a minor celebrity in Pocatello and it was no secret to those in local basketball circles that his young assistant was a hot prospect. High school athletic directors in less populous states have always turned to local colleges for assistance in finding quality coaches for their programs. To Butler's amazement, he received a number of unexpected offers to teach and coach from high schools throughout Idaho. He wondered if he should respond. He was planning to find a job in California that summer but the fact of the matter was there was no guarantee he would, especially after what he went through the previous summer. *Why not interview for some of these jobs at least?*

Butler picked up a letter of recommendation from Grayson, who would be moving on to the University of Washington soon anyway, as it turned out. With mimeographed copies of that letter he seriously applied for some of the more ideal jobs he'd been offered. His resume looked good. He'd been a volunteer assistant at Oklahoma University, a high school head coach for three years, plus he had the year experience as a Division I assistant. Not many 28 year olds could boast that! *If I can just get a job, I'll bet I can convince Sharon to move.*

To abbreviate matters, everything fell into place. Butler's first interview secured him the head basketball and tennis coach jobs at Twin Falls High School in Twin Falls, Idaho, where he beat out some rather stiff competition based on the strength of his youthful resume and glowing recommendation from Grayson. An Idaho favorite son (Butler can't remember his name but it sounded something like the name of the comic strip character "Buzz Canyon"), the best athlete to come out of Idaho in recent years, was one candidate vying for the job, while the other applicant of note was Dick Motta, who eventually coached the Chicago Bulls in the NBA. Motta sat outside the principal's office grumbling and complaining the whole time about what a waste of time it was for him to interview. He got on Butler's nerves. The other guy was very polite and as personable as anyone Butler had ever met. Butler was sure they'd select him since he was such a popular athlete in Idaho. However, Butler out-interviewed both finalists. Besides coaching he would also teach college prep biology. Now all he had to do was convince Sharon to marry him and move to Idaho.

TWIN FALLS

Ollie Butler's fourth summer working at Disneyland truly took him to the happiest place on earth. On August 23, 1959, he married Sharon Ann LaBonte in Santa Ana, California. The new Mr. And Mrs. Butler honeymooned in the mountain resort of Big Bear Lake, California, and the following week they were on the road to Idaho. Sharon had agreed to give Twin Falls a try.

Twin Falls was a homogenous community. Folks were polite and respectful. As in Pocatello, the community was nearly all white and primarily the same religion: Mormon. There was only one drawback, Sharon was Catholic.

Ollie was hired for $4,700 a year, a fortune compared to his previous year's penury as a graduate assistant for $50 a month. He and his new bride were financially quite comfortable. They rented a house in the heart of town for $90 a month. Butler dug in and went to work. He wasn't lonely or homesick a bit, he fit right in, making friends quickly and adapting to the Twin Falls environment the same way he had adapted everywhere else he lived since he left Tennessee. Fitting in wasn't as easy for Sharon.

Always practical though, Sharon understood the dynamics of her situation. She was in a new environment with a new husband and she didn't have much to do with her time. Cognitively she understood it would take time to get to know people and make friends. There was a small Catholic community that would undoubtedly open up some social opportunities eventually. Ollie would make friends with some of his co-workers and she'd get to meet them and their families. But until she got settled in better, Sharon figured she'd take matters in hand and get back into college classes and pursue her undergraduate degree in history. This would keep her occupied and her mind focused on something other than her loneliness for her family and California friends. It was a good plan, that is until she had a little visit from the stork.

Instead of returning to college, Sharon stuck close to home and spent a lot of time helping Ollie grading papers and preparing lesson plans. It was okay with her. She had been raised in a traditional Catholic family. She didn't have huge career aspirations at that time. Being a "homemaker" was still considered a respectable profession. She'd finish college later, once she got her kids in school.

Sharon settled down into her pregnancy and whiled away the hours Ollie was at work. In the evenings they would take walks and on the weekends they would go for picnics and to the movies. They were both avid

47

readers. The time actually started to fly by. And then along came the greatest time-consuming device in the history of man's progression: television. By 1960 every decent middle-class home in America had one. How could anyone feel lonely with TV to inform and entertain? This was a distraction Sharon enjoyed. Ollie also introduced Sharon to a couple of his co-worker's wives and to some of the ladies who worked in the school district office. Sharon got Ollie to attend church with her regularly on Sunday. By January of 1960, Sharon was feeling more comfortable.

There was another source of entertainment for Sharon too: Ollie's coaching. She loved to watch him, but soon wondered how such a mild-mannered Southern gentleman could become transformed so quickly into an animated madman on the sidelines of a basketball court. She hadn't seen that side of his personality before. Her initial reaction was to slide down behind some people sitting in front of her and pretend she didn't know Ollie. However, it didn't take her long to figure out that as a coach he also needed to be entertaining. She realized some of his antics were merely affective. When he coached the tennis team his demeanor was altogether different—low-key, cool, calm, subdued. He never raised his voice at a match. Of course there were never a thousand screaming fans at the tennis matches like there were at the basketball games. There was only one incident having to do with the tennis team that rankled Sharon.

Once, when she was about seven months pregnant and out in the back yard caked with dirt while working in the garden, two of Ollie's senior varsity tennis players dropped by looking like young fashion models. They loved their coach and just wanted to say "Hi!" while passing through the neighborhood. Sharon stood there looking like a pot-bellied scarecrow in her overalls and straw hat trying to act natural while the two girls bantered with her husband. It was a while before she forgave him for bringing the girls into the back yard for introductions.

At the end of Ollie's first year at Twin Falls High, where his basketball team went 16-6 and his tennis team ran a close race for the league title, Ollie promised to take Sharon home to see her family for the summer. She couldn't return to her job at Disneyland though like he could, she had a new full-time job. On May 30, 1960, the first of the Butler's four children, Jana Lynn, was born.

Ollie called up his old bosses, Dick Nunez and Ron Dominguez, as soon as they got into town. They had a spot all lined up for him. This was Butler's fifth summer working at Disneyland and he said, "If it weren't for basketball summer leagues and camps, I would have worked at Disneyland every summer for the rest of my life. It was that much fun."

Near summer's end, Sharon became reluctant about returning to Idaho. It felt so good to be back home with family and friends. However, she knew her duty was to support her husband. To make Twin Falls more palatable though, she approached Ollie about buying another new innovation in American technology: a mobile home. (Hint-hint, the key word is "mobile.") Mobile homes were becoming trendy in the late 1950s and early 1960s. The term "trailer trash" hadn't been coined yet. The honeymooning couple, Lucy and Ricky, had popularized them in the 1954 movie, "The Long, Long Trailer."

When Ollie, Sharon and baby Jana got back to Twin Falls, Sharon found a nearly new 43 foot mobile home for sale. A young couple planning to adopt a baby and move into a new home wanted to sell it. It was an excellent buy at $6,500. Square footage-wise it was as big as the small house they'd rented the previous year. (Plus, hint-hint again, this home could be moved and later sold. Sharon, who had taken over the financial accounts for the family from Ollie, had a plan.)

In his second season at Twin Falls, Butler's basketball team went 12-8 and won the district championship, before going to the state tournament, while his tennis team again vied for the league title. The athletic director and principal were quite pleased with their selection of Butler as head coach. For too many years the basketball program had languished. Now it had been revived with two consecutive trips to the playoffs. The whole community, it seemed, was taking quite a little shine to this transplanted Tennessean. Most of Butler's players were Mormon boys. He said of them, "They were some of the hardest working players I had in all my years of coaching."

But at home, with a new child and a homesick young wife, it was looking less and less like there would be a "next year" at Twin Falls for Ollie. Sharon just wasn't happy, as brave and supportive as she tried to be, and Ollie could feel a domestic tenseness mounting. "Our children," Sharon mentioned less than nonchalantly one Sunday afternoon in April of 1961, "will never know their grandparents, aunts, uncles and cousins if we continue to live so far away." To stay in Twin Falls would amount to a lifetime exile from all the things she wanted to do. At least that's how she felt then. So Butler did the only sensible thing a man can do in that situation, he resigned and vowed to find a job in California.

Ollie packed up the family and took them all to Orange County for the summer again. They would find a place near Sharon's parents in Santa Ana. Sharon had actually been raised in San Bernardino, or "Berdoo" as the locals abbreviated it. She'd attended Catholic school at St. Bernadine's. Most of her friends still lived there. She'd only moved to Santa Ana the year she met Ollie because her father had taken a job at IBM.

Once in California, Ollie again got reinstated for his sixth summer at Disneyland. This would be his last summer working there though he didn't know it at the time. He was hoping a summer at home with her family and near her friends would replenish Sharon's spirits and that by the end of summer she'd be willing to leave with him again to wherever he found work, but by mid-summer it was apparent that wasn't going to be the case. Sharon wanted to stay local, somewhere right near Santa Ana, but so far Ollie had only applied to school districts further away in the Los Angles area. Eventually he put in his resumes throughout Orange County, but when nothing had turned up by late July, Sharon suggested he also apply for teaching and coaching jobs around the Inland Empire area—her childhood stomping grounds: San Bernardino, Redlands, Fontana, Rialto, Bloomington, Rancho Cucamonga, Grand Terrace, Norco, Corona, Riverside, Colton, Yucaipa, even the High Desert as a last resort. And so Butler did, but only half-heartedly. He figured something was likely to turn up in the LA area in August. School districts were like that, sometimes they didn't know how many teachers they'd need until just before the start of school. He had faith.

Toward early August Sharon dug in her heels. She was adamant about Ollie finding a job nearby so she could raise the children around family. She questioned whether he was really trying to find a job near Santa Ana. This time he hit the application circuit with more energy, feeling he was fighting a battle he couldn't win. He followed up on the applications he had already sent out to Santa Ana, Fullerton, Fountain Valley, Newport Beach, Costa Mesa, Long Beach and elsewhere. He also sent out another stack of resumes, this time to some of the outlying districts of the Inland Empire, then safely escaped each afternoon to the fantasy world of Disneyland.

In mid-August Butler got a call from Victorville, on the edge of the Mojave Desert, a place Sharon once called "God-forsaken" when she passed through it on a train trip home over Christmas vacation the year before. There was an opening for a job teaching science and coaching at a junior high. Did he want to come in and interview?

VICTORVILLE—THE BEGINNING

Ollie Butler never wanted to leave his job at Twin Falls but he realized that Sharon needed the bosom of family, relatives and friends. More importantly, he needed Sharon. Now that they were back in Santa Ana, Ollie liked how at ease she was. He knew she would be miserable if he put her through another year away from everyone. It was obvious that if he wanted to appease his wife he had to find a teaching job in Southern California soon. But Victorville? It wasn't exactly Orange County!

When he told Sharon about the offer she echoed his own sentiments. "Victorville! Are you kidding me? Who would want to live out there?" What she saw from the train window the previous year told her all she needed to know: lizards, snakes, scorpions, jackrabbits, a vast dusty-brown windswept landscape, dry heat, sparse vegetation of tumbleweeds, sage and greasewood, and for shade, the Joshua tree. Only Death Valley could be more remote! No thanks! However, the reality was, she'd probably settle for Victorville if she had to. It was, after all, only 80 minutes away from her family in Santa Ana, a lot closer than Idaho.

Butler was not too keen on the idea either, especially since the Victor Valley Unified High School District's job offer was to teach and coach at Imogene Garner-Hook Junior High. What he wanted was a high school job teaching history and a varsity basketball program to run. When he mentioned this in the interview, Superintendent Harvey Irwin took him aside and made Butler a verbal offer. The offer was that if Butler would put in one year at the junior high level, Irwin would get him promoted to the high school the following year, where he would teach history and take over the varsity basketball program. *Should I take the chance?*

When Irwin presented this offer to Butler he was skeptical at first. Not knowing Irwin, how could he be sure this would happen? However, the summer would soon be ending and this was the only solid offer he had that would keep his family in California. Besides being close to Santa Ana, Victorville was also only three hours away from Las Vegas. Butler, like a feverish Vegas gambler, considered the stakes, calculated the odds, placed his bet, blew on the dice and made his come out roll. He signed the contract. If Irwin followed through on his promise to get him the varsity basketball program, the gamble to move to Victorville could pay huge dividends. They sealed their verbal deal the old fashioned way, with a handshake. Butler had nothing in writing but he trusted Irwin to make it happen. The trust, it turned out, was well placed.

Butler hired a young man Irwin recommended to drive to Twin Falls in his truck and haul their mobile home trailer to Victorville. (Remember the hint?) When he arrived with it they discovered the 43 foot trailer was too big to fit into any of the trailer parks in Victorville. They had to take it to the neighboring Village of Apple Valley, where they lived in it for one year, until their second daughter was born.

Meanwhile, Harvey Irwin went to work on his plan to bring the talented and highly regarded basketball coach, Ollie Butler, to Victor Valley High. Neal Case was currently the head basketball and baseball coach at Victor Valley. Case was a good baseball coach but not a very good basketball coach. Superintendent Irwin wanted a better basketball program to represent the school district, so did Keith Gunn, principal of Victor Valley High. Gunn had coached the basketball team for many years before moving up into administration. Ever since he had left the program it had declined. When Harvey Irwin told Gunn about Butler and the offer he made him, Gunn knew just what to do, convince Case to devote more time to baseball and consider giving up the basketball program. He had one year to do it and he didn't think it would be too hard since Case had only taken on the basketball program as a favor to Gunn because no one else on the staff at the time was qualified to run it.

By the end of the 1961-62 school year, Gunn had done his work well. Case resigned the head basketball job to spend more time focusing on his first love—baseball. Low and behold, there was an opening for a head basketball coach at Victor Valley High, and qualified candidates who worked in the school district would be considered first. Ollie Butler was a qualified candidate who worked in the district.

Meanwhile, at Hook Junior High, Butler spent the 1961-62 school year teaching science and P.E. He coached three sports: football, basketball, and track. Figuring he would be moving up to the high school the following year, Butler kept an ever vigilant scouting-eye out for future varsity basketball prospects. He was looking for athletic kids. From Grayson at Idaho State, Butler had learned a few recruiting techniques, the primary one being something Grayson may have borrowed from Dale Carnegie's *How to Win Friends and Influence People*: show a genuine interest in others.

Butler showed an interest by making it a point to talk to the boys about sports whenever he could. Most boys like one sport or another. He wanted to find out what sport they liked the most and who their heroes were. They talked about the local Southern California teams: the Rams, the Lakers and the Dodgers. In his two P. E. classes, Butler had an opportunity to see who had speed, quickness, agility and stamina. In his three science classes he could assess who had brains and the ability to listen and learn. Often he would get up a baseball game on the school's diamond for anyone who wanted to play during lunch or after school. He was always scouting, but the kids were also scouting him. Steve Scoggin, who was in Butler's 7th grade science class, remembered how impressed he was by Butler's hitting skills in their pick-up baseball games. "He could hit the ball any where he wanted to. We could never get him out." Butler knew from past experience that a coach who could play ball well would gain the kids' respect.

By the time his year at Hook was finished Butler knew who all the top athletes were who would be moving up from Hook to Victor Valley High School in the next few years. But what about the district's other school, Victor Valley Junior High? He needed to scout those kids too. To do this he would have to apply another of Grayson's recruiting strategies: go see them play in their element.

Though Butler coached at Hook, his basketball team practiced across town at Victor Junior High. Why didn't they practice at their own gym? They didn't have one, they had a hybrid-cafeteria. Butler refused to make his team practice in the Hook cafeteria where the school district had ingeniously installed baskets to save the expense of building a gym. The floor was tiled making the floor slippery, not to mention that after lunch every day it got coated with spilled food and sticky drinks that the custodians seldom cleaned up thoroughly enough for Butler's liking. Butler insisted that his team practice on a proper hard wood floor. Superintendent Irwin saw to it that Butler got practice time in the Victor Junior High gym.

Butler's ninth grade team (back then junior high was seventh through ninth grades and high school was tenth through twelfth) started practice at 4:30, right after Victor Junior finished theirs. In his role as scout, Butler would show up early under the pretense of sitting in the stands to write up his practice plan, but what he was really doing was watching Victor Junior's practices and checking out the talent pool. These boys would also be moving up to Victor Valley High. Butler wanted to know what kind of players he'd have coming from this side of town.

Butler became good friends with Victor Junior coach, Danny Ribbons. Ribbons knew Butler wasn't keeping his eye strictly on his practice plans, but he didn't care. Ribbons was a strong coach himself. It would give him that much more satisfaction to beat Butler's Hook team, knowing that Butler had been able to scout and prepare for them. Ribbons had no idea that Butler was actually looking ahead, planning combinations of athletes from both Hook and Victor that would work next year when he would take over the basketball program at the high school. In fact, if Danny Ribbons had known about Harvey Irwin's offer to Butler, he would have been up in arms. Ribbons wanted to move up to the high school and coach there too. When the position did open up, Danny Ribbons was Butler's primary competition, since he was another qualified coach already teaching in the district. Unfortunately for Ribbons, he didn't have the resume Butler had.

One afternoon, on his way to Victor Junior before practice, Butler decided to drop by the high school and see what Case was doing with his team and get a peak at the players' work ethic in practice. Butler knew who the players were who'd be returning next year. He was a regular at Victor Valley High School basketball games. Out of those players he already knew who was talented and who could be developed, who had attitudes, and who looked easy to coach, but seeing them at practice would give him further insight—another Grayson technique.

Butler walked into the Quonset hut shaped Victor Valley High gym unannounced. He leaned against the wall just inside the double-doors leading from the foyer into the gym. This would soon be Butler's home away from home. He wanted to get a feel for it in the afternoon, since he'd soon be spending countless hours of his time there preparing his players in practice. Butler was the kind of coach who loved practices.

Butler liked this gym. (At the time the gym had no name, but later in Butler's career it would be named after principal Keith Gunn, in honor of Gunn's many years at Victor Valley as a teacher, coach and principal.) It was small. Maybe 800-1000 people could crowd in. The wooden bleachers (ten benches high) were close to the court, which would make the crowd noise that much louder and more intense. There were four side baskets making for two practice full-courts side by side. An odd thing Butler noticed right away was that the main court floor seemed shorter. Later he found out it was indeed 10 feet shorter than regulation—a contractor's boondoggle when the gym was originally built. (Butler calculated this would give the home team an added trapping advantage on defense, since opponents would come in thinking they had the usual regulation 94 feet to work in, when in fact they only had 84 feet.)

Case and another man were at mid-court with their backs to Butler. Beyond them the varsity was using the far half court to practice, if you could call it that. To Butler, it appeared that "Case didn't coach. The players just fooled around shooting and hacking at one another while Case stood joking with the other man, though he did occasionally holler at the team." According to Butler's time frame, he'd walked in on what should have been the heart of practice time. He didn't like what he saw. These boys were going to have their eyes opened next year to what a real practice was. Unimpressed, he turned around and walked out. Case never knew he was there.

In March of 1962, Neal Case tendered his resignation as basketball coach. By late April, the qualified candidates to replace him had all gone through the interview process. In mid-May, Victor Valley High announced that Ollie Butler had been named the new varsity basketball coach. Right away, this angered some people. *Who was this new guy? What about Danny Ribbons?*

No one was more upset than the Victor Junior High ninth grade boys basketball team. Willie Ray McDonald, who would later become a close friend of Butler's as well as a colleague and his long-time assistant coach, was a member of that team. He told me in a fortuitous interview—one week before he shocked us all and died of a heart attack at 54—that the Victor Junior players were considering a boycott of Butler's program. They had convinced themselves that they wouldn't get a fair tryout. They thought that Butler would show favoritism to his former players from Hook Junior. They also felt Danny Ribbons should have been selected as the head coach because he had been around longer. Fortunately, by the time tryout's came around the following October, they had simmered down and changed their minds. Quickly they found out their imagined favoritism couldn't have been further from the truth. Butler had learned under John Grayson what a detriment it was to a program to play favorites. McDonald said, "Ollie Butler turned out to be the fairest of all the coaches I ever played for."

Another milestone took place in Butler's life along about the time he was being announced as Victor Valley High's newest basketball coach. Ollie and Sharon's second daughter, Rebecca Ann, was born on May 12, 1962. The long, long trailer got a little shorter, sending Sharon to work shopping for homes.

In Victorville, just up the street from Victor Valley High, a brand new tract of homes was being finished. The tract was called Tatum Plaza, after the Tatums, a potato farming family turned land developers. Sharon picked out a new home on Laguna Street to show to Ollie. He liked it. Within days Sharon sold the mobile home to a young trailer court magnate named Doris Davies (a woman who needs no introduction to long time residents of Victorville). Sharon sold the mobile home for the same price they paid for it, giving the Butler's, in essence, free rent for the past two years. They used the money for a down payment on the Laguna Street home, six blocks from Ollie's new place of employment. It was a good investment. They still live in it today, 40 years later.

Butler was extremely busy that June. He had to wind up his year at Hook, move his family into their new home and institute his new summer basketball program—a tradition that would run for the next three decades. The gym would be opened, once school let out, every afternoon in June and July, Monday through Friday, from one to five. All junior high and high school aged boys were welcome at the open-gym as long as they abided by the rules (rules he brought with him from Forrest Brooks' YMCA in Tennessee): no profanity or vulgarity, no fighting, no full-court games—

only three on three half court games, and you had to sit out after your team won two games in a row to let other teams have their shot.

Victor Valley had a real basketball coach again. A new era had begun, an era that would last for 28 years.

VICTOR VALLEY HIGH—1962-64

Keith Gunn, now entering his 13th year as principal, welcomed and introduced Butler at the general staff meeting prior to the start of the 1962-63 school year. The campus was still fairly new and was built to accommodate about 1000 students. Twin Falls High was approximately the same size, but there was a big difference in the student population. Unlike the other places Butler had taught and coached at, Victorville had an ethnically diverse population. In Tennessee, Oklahoma and Idaho, whites and minorities were still pretty well segregated. Prior to coming to Victorville, Butler hadn't taught Asian, African, and Latino Americans before. Victorville was like the United Nations compared to where he'd come from.

Butler immediately liked this heterogeneous mix. In the military he'd experienced integration and liked meeting people of different ethnic and racial backgrounds. At Hook Junior High he'd taught minorities for the first time and found kids of color to be just that, kids, no different because of skin color. Yet in 1962, America still had a predominantly racist mentality, generally speaking, even in liberal California, though luckily the racist component of American culture was being challenged.

Dr. Martin Luther King Jr., chosen to advance the cause of equality by virtue of his leadership during the Montgomery bus boycott in 1955-56, was raising people's consciousness about race discrimination throughout the nation. The Civil Rights Movement was in full swing. Butler, a liberal in his politics and a proponent of socially progressive movements, was glad to be in California where people were more tolerant and broadminded. Unfortunately, Butler was to find out, California was not Nirvana. There were intolerant and small-minded people in Victorville the same as there were everywhere else, and some of them were even teachers.

"There was a lot of latent racism when I first started teaching and coaching at Victor Valley," Butler said. "Some of it was open, too. There were a few teachers who used the "N" word right in the teacher's workroom. There were coaches who used derogatory racial epithets out loud on the practice fields." On occasion, overt racism entered the classroom. Butler remembered being told by some of his students that a colleague in the English department told a group of talkative African-American kids in the back row of her class to, "Be quiet you jig boos."

Not only did Butler see this ugly form of racial prejudice practiced by individuals, he also saw it institutionally. At the high school level many non-white students consistently ended up in vocational programs rather than in academic ones. With few exceptions, only white kids took chemistry, physics, algebra, calculus and college-prep literature courses. Butler noted this in his early tenure at Victor Valley and determined he would be a part of changing this inequitable pattern.

Adversity can be a great stimulus for change. The 1960s was a time of great social revolution in America and Victor Valley High School became a microcosm of that upheaval. Butler learned how to teach well because of societal adversity. If you were in Butler's history class as a student, you knew he wasn't just some jock coach. He was a real student of the subject himself. He did his homework. He came to class well-prepared. To Butler, teaching history was as fun and stimulating as coaching basketball, in fact, to him they were the very same thing.

In the classroom, Butler taught everyone: the good students, the bad students and the indifferent students. He engaged them with social issues and made history relevant. Racial prejudice, for example, might be an issue dividing many people in the country, but Butler did not shy away from discussing it in his classroom. And to his teaching credit, it was never an issue that divided his classroom, in fact, the dialogues usually brought people closer together.

Butler didn't limit his zeal for academics to the classroom though, something his basketball players soon found out. After school in the gym, Butler continued to stress to his players that they put into their classes the same energy they put into basketball. He gave as many lectures about the importance of education as he did about the correct way to shoot a free throw. He also went to see the counselors about getting his minority players into academic classes. Butler preferred his student-athletes to attain college scholarships based on intellectual prowess rather than on athletic ability alone.

Butler's first basketball season at Victor Valley High School (which I will frequently abbreviate to VVHS from this time forward) was memorable. The "Jacks," as the school mascot Jackrabbits were then diminutively called in the old *Victor Press*, jumped out to a 9-0 record. True, they were playing small schools like themselves—Twenty-nine Palms, Yucca Valley, Needles and the like, but nine wins against no losses is always respectable no matter who you are playing. Once league began though they met stiffer competition.

The Jackrabbits went 4-4 in Golden League play. They beat the schools their size—Ridgecrest and Barstow, but lost to the bigger schools— Antelope Valley and Palmdale. They finished third in a five team league and did not go to the playoffs. (You had to finish first to go to the playoffs then, not like today's politically and economically correct let's-not-let-the-underachieving-teams-have-a-low-self-esteem-mentality that sends every team to the playoffs practically. (Get this, just last season a team with a record of 6-16 played in the wildcard game of the CIF playoffs. And what do you think happened? They got scorched by 47 points. I don't know how that helped their morale, but it did bring in ticket revenues to the school, which has become the real name of the game. Mediocrity pays! But I digress, forgive me.)

The Jackrabbits finished their first season under Butler with an overall record of 15-4. The numbers sound impressive. Not a bad start for a new coach, you'd think. But Butler was in no way satisfied. He wanted a league title and he wanted it right away.

In Butler's second season, he got something many coaches never get in an entire career; the Jackrabbits went all the way to the CIF semifinals. VVHS had never gone that far into the playoffs before, even when the stalwart Keith Gunn was coaching them. The 1963-64 team was the fruition of Butler's coaching and scouting at Hook and Victor Junior High. Butler had brought these boys along the way he knew he could, and the best part was that the better athletes on the team were only juniors with another season to go.

Despite their huge accomplishment, the 1963-64 season did not start out very well. Coach Butler had a hard time focusing on basketball and so did his players. America's thoughts were on something far more serious.

On Nov. 22, 1963, Fella Scoggin walked into Butler's American history classroom just after lunch and announced that President Kennedy had been shot but he was going to be okay. Butler thought Scoggin was playing another of his practical jokes and admonished him for jesting in such poor taste. Dixie Riley, class of 1965, and later a colleague of Butler's at VVHS, was in that class and never forgot what happened next: "A little after Fella sat down," Riley recounted, "Tony Balsamo, the athletic director, came over the crackly intercom—I still get chills whenever an intercom crackles—and announced that Governor John Connally of Texas had been shot and wounded and that President Kennedy had been assassinated while riding in a motorcade in preparation for re-election. Mr. Butler slowly began to shake his head from side to side in disbelief, then tears started to stream down his face. A few moments later he laid his head down on his desk. It was only the second time in my life I'd ever seen a grown man cry and it made an unforgettable impression on me."

That was one of the few times Butler ever cancelled practice and it was no wonder that a couple weeks later when the season began no one was in very high spirits.

The 1963-64 team was led by a host of juniors. Bob Jones, who would make All-CIF at forward and go on to play for the University of Pacific, was joined by fellow juniors Fella Scoggin, who started at guard, Willie Ray McDonald, who started at the other forward, plus back up swing-man Roy Dell White and sharp-shooter guard Mike Musgrave. Only two seniors started: center Ron Jones and guard Kenny Gross—who sometimes traded starting spots with the speedy Hector Ramirez. These were about the only players Butler used all season. (It wouldn't be until the mid-Seventies that Butler would develop his philosophy of using a deep bench to wear teams down.)

The 1963-64 squad went 11-1 in preseason, which they followed with a 7-1 league run, losing only to powerhouse Antelope Valley in a 65-64 knuckle-biter. They took first place and finished the regular season 18-2; then came the CIF playoffs and their surprising surge toward the championship game.

The CIF (California Interscholastic Federation) playoffs are the equivalent of the Sectionals and Regionals in other states. In the first round, VVHS earned a bye based on their outstanding record. In the second round, they beat La Salle 75-73, at home in overtime, when Kenny Gross calmly sank two free throws with 10 seconds to go. In the quarterfinals, VVHS used a full-court press the entire game to wear down perennial Catholic school champion Mater Dei. Leading by 7 at the end of the third quarter, Butler went into his patented delay-game, forcing mater Dei to foul to stop the clock. Fella Scoggin hit nine straight foul shots and VVHS won 60-49. Back-up forward Roy Dell White pulled down 14 rebounds while playing less than half the game. But Victor Valley's hopes of winning a CIF title were dashed when Lausen, coached by former Seattle University's Al Brightman, neutralized Victor's inside game with their big center Mike Halligan. (And by the way, what was a big time college coach doing back in the high school ranks?) Halligan dominated the boards and scored 30 points in Lausen's win. They won the CIF title in their next game. Halligan went on to play at Stanford and eventually became a doctor.

The good news was that the 1963-64 team overachieved and that most of the team would be back as seniors next year. Furthermore, Butler had some strong players coming up off the lower-level teams who would round out a talented bunch of returning playoff-tested lettermen. VVHS looked as if it had a pretty good shot at that CIF championship next season.

VVHS: THE 1964-65 SEASON

"Greg Hyder is a big black nigger," read the epithet on the locker room chalkboard as the varsity players filed in from another exhausting preseason practice. Having won the Golden League crown the previous season, then powering all the way to the semifinals in the playoffs, Butler wasn't about to let up on conditioning, a factor he attributed to much of last season's success. Until about mid-season his players would characteristically drag themselves out of the gym and into the locker room after each practice. "If they weren't dragging," Butler said, "I knew I hadn't work them hard enough."

It was Friday, the day after Thanksgiving, Nov. 27, 1964, and VVHS, the small 2A school on the outskirts of civilization—at least that's where the teams who drove out from Orange County said it was—was going into the season ranked number one following their strong 1963-64 march to the semifinals. Butler was beginning his tenth year of coaching and never before had a season looked so promising at the outset.

It wasn't just the fact that he had a talented bunch of returning lettermen that portended good tidings, there was another light in Butler's eye, a special gift from his wife. On October 1, 1964, Sharon brought their third precious daughter into the world, Catherine Ellen Butler. With three girls Butler felt he was a lucky man. He knew if he raised these girls well, they'd be devoted to him for life. Whimsically, he began looking forward to teaching Jana, Becky and Cathy how to keep stats for him.

The varsity was returning three starters and two experienced back up players. The other players rounding out the roster were all strong too. Butler told Mike Girard of *The Victor Press* in an interview the Tuesday before Thanksgiving that, "These are the best 15 boys I've ever had." Talk of a CIF title for VVHS was also in the air. The prognosticators felt they had the quickness, the size, the shooting and the defense necessary to go all the way. Still, for Butler, it was too early to gauge the pulse of this team. They had only practiced so far. Their first scrimmage wasn't scheduled until the following week and their first game wouldn't be until the second week in December. Yet, Butler was optimistic that his returners would jell with the newcomers and this would become a strong squad. Until this.

"All right, who wrote that up there?" questioned a scarlet-faced Butler glaring menacingly at the team now assembled before him in front of the chalkboard. Racism was a rude ignorance Butler despised.

No one had access to the locker room during practice. Butler ran the proverbial "tight ship." Each day, about five minutes after practice commenced, Butler locked the exterior doors and sealed the gym tighter than a submarine at fifty fathoms. No distractions were permitted by interlopers. Even Keith Gunn—Butler's favorite boss in all his years at Victor Valley, though Don Conde was a close second—was looked at askance if he was audacious enough to let himself in with his own master key to observe practice.

Someone on the team had to have written this slur. No one else has been in here. The C and B team practices aren't scheduled until later in the day. School's out so no one else could have slipped in. No, this is an inside job, and if I don't do something about it right now a division like this could pull the team apart faster than I can say Jackrabbits.

"I mean it! I want to know who wrote this up here. If you tell me now you won't be kicked off the team, but if I find out later…let me rephrase that…when I find out later, not only will you be removed from this team immediately but I will personally see to it that you don't play another sport at this school again!"

Silence. An interminable moment of silence. Then…

"Ah rote it Coach," an embarrassed Roy Dell White confessed, "but I wuz jus' messn 'round. We always call each other that."

Butler sighed an inaudible breath of relief. *Thank God. At least one of the white players didn't write it.*

The nation was currently embroiled in a struggle for civil rights. Martin Luther King Jr. had just won a Noble Peace Prize in October for his leadership in the non-violent struggle against racial discrimination. His "I Have a Dream" speech, given before a quarter million protest marchers on August 23, 1963, had polarized a troubled country divided by color lines. Butler, the new resident liberal at VVHS, was a big King supporter. An anomaly from the cottin' pickin' South, where racism and segregation were still a way of life, Butler, strangely had never been infected by the poison of racism. And now, in ethnically diverse Southern California, he was facing this ignorance scrawled on the locker room play-board. This was an affront he could not tolerate, but, it was also a teachable moment if he handled it right.

"Roy Dell," Butler began, "I don't ever want to hear you use that word again. Not at school! Not at home! Not on the streets! Not anywhere! It's an ignorant person's word. You're smarter than that. And that goes for the rest of you too! That word is degrading, shameful and humiliating. Pin-headed whites came up with that word and anyone who uses it is ignorant. I won't stand for small-minded players on this team. Do you all understand me?"

Later, Butler was actually glad the season started so dramatically. More than anything else, Butler wanted to make a difference in the world.

Growing up poor during the Depression had impressed him with a driving desire to make something of himself. If he could get these high school kids to see beyond the superficiality of race, perhaps they would go on to help stamp out discrimination and prejudice for good and he would have had a hand in it. Now that would be an accomplishment!

Though I am not supposed to tell anyone, the 1964-65 Jackrabbit squad was Butler's favorite team in all his years of coaching. He felt they had no weaknesses. "They were big, strong and ugly," Butler remembers. "Girls are never as big a distraction when the players are ugly. I think that's why we did so well."

The Rabbits steam-rolled through their pre-league schedule. They went 12-2 but both losses were extremely close. Senior forward Bob Jones made the All-Kiwanis team at the San Bernardino Christmas tournament. Then, their winning ways continued in league play. Again, the Jackrabbits repeated as Golden League Champs—this time going 8-0. When the time came for the CIF playoff bracketings, the Rabbits were seeded number one.

With the experience Victor Valley had from last year's playoffs, coupled with their 20-2 record, their confidence was high, so when the pairings came out and they were matched up against a tough inner-city school, Servite, they didn't bat an eye. No one intimidated them. Secretly though, Butler was worried. He'd seen Servite play and knew this was a tough first round draw even though the teams paralleled each other in so many ways. Both had big centers, quick point-guards and outside streak-shooters. Each had athletic forwards who could score inside and talented back-up players to replace them. Both teams were known for their smothering defense.

"Tight, is the way I'd describe this game," Butler recalled. "The lead see-sawed back and forth throughout the game and neither team could pull away. Both squads played tremendous defense. We were very evenly matched."

With less than a minute to go, Victor went up by one, 59-58. All they had to do was stop Servite one more time. Servite's point-guard cautiously brought the ball up court against pressure from Fella Scoggin. He passed it to the shooting guard on the perimeter guarded by Mike Musgrave. After a couple of perimeter passes one of the guards entered the ball to the post. Servite's center put up a bank shot that missed badly and rebounded hard off the glass. Both teams went for the rebound but no one could control it. In a surrealistic moment that Butler has replayed countless times in his mind, the ball was slapped and swatted repeatedly without anyone controlling possession, until cosmic irony (the dice of the basketball gods are loaded) kicked in with little time left on the clock.

Butler had instructed his inside players day in and day out at practice that if they couldn't grab a rebound outright they were to tip it against the backboard to keep it alive for another try. Bob Jones was just a little too good at this technique. Unable to grab the rebound himself against Servite's center, Jones kept batting the ball against the backboard like Butler had taught him. Unfortunately, with precious seconds left to go, he accidentally tapped it in to Servite's basket, giving them a 60-59 lead.

Time out!

Coolly, Butler designed a game-winning play in the team huddle. Bob Jones, Fella Scoggin and Mike Musgrave were all having a big night. Butler drew up options that would give any one of these guys an opportunity to take the last shot, though the first option was for Musgrave to come off a Jones pick, catch a pass from Scoggin and shoot an open perimeter jump shot—his best shot.

Time in!

In comes the ball and up the court dribbles Scoggin…10…9…8…the clock ticks down. Jones sets his pick and Musgrave circles around to scrape off it…7…6…5…Scoggin, after faking a pass one direction to McDonald comes back the other direction with a perfect pass to Musgrave who catches it, turns, faces the basket…4…3…2…and shoots…1…It's good!

Oops, no it's not…it's in and out, it's rolling around the rim while the game-ending buzzer is sounding…it's in…out…in…then out as the ball rolls off the rim and drops to the floor. No good!

Victor Valley, the number one ranked team, loses 60-59 in the first round of the playoffs. Their only consolation is that Servite sweeps to the CIF title and no one else really gives them a game.

Butler took the loss hard, especially since he knew it was his bat-the-ball-against-the- backboard-until-you-can-control-it technique that put Jones in the unenviable position of accidentally tipping the ball in for the other team to win. However, Butler did not let anyone see how bad he felt. Neal Case, Butler's predecessor at VVHS, was in the locker room after the loss and witnessed Butler console his players, especially Jones. Afterwards Case told Butler, "That was the best speech after a loss I've ever heard."

"What did I say?" Butler responded in a daze.

George Struebing, a junior on the 1965 team, who came back after college to teach with Ollie Butler in the History department for many years, remembered the bitterness of that defeat, but also credited Ollie Butler with bringing name recognition to Victor Valley High. Big games like this, even though the Rabbits lost, were what got people in other parts of Southern California asking *Where's Victorville?* "Ollie Butler, so to speak, put Victorville on the map," said Struebing.

Though the Jackrabbits had fallen in the playoffs two years in a row, no one was down on the Rabbits or their coach the way some fans will get. In three short years at VVHS, Butler had amassed a fine 56-11 record. If he kept up like this there was no doubt VVHS would eventually win a CIF title.

VVHS 1966-69

In comparison to what Butler's teams did in the 1964 and 1965 seasons, the rest of the decade turned out to be anticlimactic. No other teams in the 1960s advanced as far in the playoffs. This was especially disappointing to the 1965-66 Jackrabbits who boasted three future college scholarship players, including future NBA player, Greg Hyder, his speedy brother Jerry, a guard (both starred at Eastern New Mexico State), and future Whittier College forward, Steve Scoggin (Fella's younger brother). While Butler had high hopes for this team, they never rose to the level he envisioned for them.

Rounding out the 1965-66 roster was: George Struebing, Hector Gonzales, Walt Hawkins, Danny Tyree, Larry Park, Mac Green and Allen Armstrong. The team would have included Pat Douglass if he hadn't transferred to Kennedy in Barstow just before school began. According to Butler, if he had been able to retain Douglass to play guard along side Jerry Hyder, he's convinced they would have gotten to the finals.

Pat Douglass is a whole chapter in Butler's life even though Douglass never played for Butler at VVHS. You may have heard about Douglass. He's been a college head coach for twenty years now and currently has a college record of 430-175. He won three NCAA Division II titles at Cal State Bakersfield, where he became the winningest coach in Bakersfield history. He was 257-61 in 10 seasons with the Roadrunners. Now he's at UC Irvine, and in four years there he totally turned around the program that went 1-25 the year before he took over. They won the Big West Conference championship last year with a 15-1 record and Douglass was named the Coach of the Year. However, when Douglass met Butler in the summer of 1964, he was just a new kid in town, having migrated out with his family from his native Tennessee prior to starting the ninth grade.

As local legend has it, Douglass went looking for the gym soon after he signed up for American Legion summer baseball, within his first week of hitting town. Like Butler, who also grew up on sports in Tennessee, Douglass lived baseball and basketball. When he got to the high school gym, after dribbling a basketball the few blocks down the street from his new house, he asked the first guy he saw in the parking lot, "What time does the coach open the gym?"

The guy he asked was Butler, who responded, "One o'clock. Who are you?"

Butler and Douglass were destined to become friends. They had the same down-home Tennessee mentality, they were two of a kind: tenacious, ultra competitive, quick and cocky. About the same size, Douglas and

66

Butler played each other one-on-one all that summer. Douglass claims that he won a number of those games. "I beat his ass many times. You can put that in your book." Butler, on the other hand, couldn't remember those losses. But what do you expect, he's in his seventies now.

If you know basketball, you know the term "gym rat." It was coined to describe people like Douglass and Butler. From the time school let out in June until the end of July, Butler opened the high school gym from 1-5 every Monday through Friday afternoon. Douglass, according to Butler, dribbled his basketball down to the high school every day it was open. Often, Butler said, "He'd be sitting on the curb dribbling the ball next to him when I got there about 12:45 to turn on the lights and dust-mop the floor. He couldn't wait to get there."

Douglass so impressed Butler with his ball-handling, shooting and quickness that he thought Douglass could start on the varsity as a sophomore. In fact, if VVHS had been a four year high school then, Douglass probably would have started as a freshman. Unfortunately, Douglass was only going into the ninth grade, so Butler did the next best thing. Before basketball season started in the fall of 1964, Butler made it a point to talk with Victor Junior High coach, Danny Ribbons, about the newcomer Douglass. Butler wanted Ribbons to work with Douglass as much as he could individually. A natural shooter, and a lefty at that, Butler hoped Douglass could give the Jackrabbits 20 points per game the following season.

His whole ninth grade season, Butler kept tabs on Douglass. He went to see him play as often as his schedule permitted. Douglass lit up the gym every time Butler saw him. At the end of the season, Butler was able to watch Douglass's performance in the ninth grade tournament featuring all the local junior highs in the Victor Valley. Douglass set a new tournament scoring record and was named Most Valuable Player. Danny Ribbons asked Butler to come down and present Douglass the trophy. It's a moment neither of them has forgotten.

In the summer of 1965, Douglass again played summer ball at VVHS and to Butler it looked certain Douglass would be in the starting line-up as a sophomore on the varsity come December. They played many more heated games of one-on-one. Butler couldn't believe how much Douglass had improved in one year. Then, towards the end of summer, Douglass brought Butler unfortunate news: he would be moving to Barstow in September to attend high school because of his father's work transfer. This directly paralleled Butler's own life story. He, too, had to leave one high school to go play at another because his father got a new job.

Douglass's departure was a huge loss to Victor Valley. Butler said, "I was so disappointed when Pat had to move. I was looking forward to him helping us tremendously." But, taking it all in stride, Butler got on the phone to an old teammate of his from the University of Oklahoma, Bill Irvin. Irvin was coaching at Kennedy High, and Butler recommended Douglass go to school there rather than Barstow High. Butler felt Irvin was a better coach than the guy at Barstow. He also wanted Douglass to play for someone he knew would help him move on to the college ranks.

After three record-setting years at Kennedy (Douglass led the state in scoring his sophomore year), in which he always had phenomenal games against VVHS, Irvin got Douglass a scholarship to the University of Pacific when he graduated in 1968. Douglass was equally successful there. Upon graduating college, Douglass became a teacher and coached high school basketball for a couple years before parlaying his talent into a highly successful career as a college basketball coach.

Still, without Douglass playing for VVHS, there were many highlights in the Jackrabbits season of 1965-66. In pre-league competition, Greg Hyder asserted himself as a dominant rebounder and shot blocker. Butler recalls Greg blocked 12 shots in one game at the San Bernardino Kiwanis Tournament, earning himself All-Tournament honors. The press write-ups in the San Bernardino papers also brought Greg a lot of attention from college recruiters. From that point on in Greg's senior year, Butler began getting a lot of calls inquiring about him.

In Golden League play, VVHS took second with a 9-3 record, but their season ended in the first round of the CIF playoffs like it had the previous season when they lost to Catholic school juggernaut, Bishop Amat. Greg Hyder, due to great season statistics, made All-CIF despite the Jackrabbits' early exit from the post season tournament. Victor Valley finished with an overall record of 15-8. But Butler's job wasn't finished, it wouldn't be until he got his talented big man into college.

Greg Hyder seemed to have unlimited athletic potential. He'd been recruited by a number of big NCAA colleges. Butler would tell recruiters, "Greg is a pro caliber player." There was only one problem, Greg's grades. He barely kept eligible all through high school and that was probably due to generosity on the part of some of his teachers who loved the big, friendly, affable Hyder and passed him along. Then there were his SATs scores—not even close. Fortunately, Butler had connections in the NAIA ranks. Those smaller colleges had a different set of rules for admittance. Butler got Hyder in at Eastern New Mexico State. Instead of being a Jackrabbit, Hyder was now a Greyhound.

Butler is quite proud of what Greg accomplished at Eastern New Mexico State. His teams went to the NAIA playoffs every season. In his junior year, joined by his brother Jerry who followed in 1967, the team won the NAIA National Championship, defeating Maryland St., who was led by

Jake Ford and M. L. Carr. In Greg's senior year, Eastern New Mexico State again made it to the final four, but finished third. However, for the first time in history, the MVP of the tournament wasn't selected from the first or even the second place team. Greg Hyder, off the third place team, won the trophy for his dominant tournament play. And for his fourth consecutive year, Greg was named All-American.

Butler was even prouder of what came next. You guessed it. The NBA. Hyder was drafted into the pros by the Cincinnati Royals (who soon after moved to Kansas City and are now the Sacramento Kings), then coached by an egotistical Bob Cousy, who Greg turned out not to like very much. When the Royals came to town to play the Los Angeles Lakers in Greg's rookie season, half of Victorville caravanned to the game. The next morning in the *Sun Telegram* there was a full size picture on the front of the sports page of Greg defending Wilt Chamberlain. Basketball fans in Greg's hometown thought they had died and gone to basketball heaven. Greg had made history by out-rebounding Wilt 13-10 and scoring 22 points. (And speaking of history, there is an exhibit of pictures at the Victor Valley Museum featuring old pioneer families of the Victor Valley. In a dusty corner there is an assortment of pictures of minority pioneer families. The Hyder family, one of Victorville's oldest families of African descent, shares a part of that exhibit. And guess who is in a few of those pictures with the Hyders? Greg's old high school coach, Ollie Butler. I like to tease Ollie about being so old he's in a museum.)

Before beginning his fifth season at VVHS, Butler was praised in *The Victor Press* for developing a "hot and fast basketball tradition" in Victorville. In that time his record had surged to 71-19. The 1966-67 Jackrabbits would do well too, surpassing by two wins the 15-8 record of last year's team. Greg Hyder's brother, Jerry, now a senior, was the locomotive force propelling the Jackrabbits. Jerry, at six foot one inch, was known as "Little Brother." Taller brothers Glen and Greg had graduated in 1964 and '66. Jerry figured to carry on the Hyder propensity for basketball drama. He did not disappoint. A fantastic ball-handler who could penetrate or pull up and shoot off the drive, he was a tremendous scorer and a terrific leaper who never failed to send the crowd into a frenzy with his acrobatic moves.

Jerry's leadership was bolstered by another little brother, Steve Scoggin, who at six foot three inches, was actually quite a bit bigger than his older brother Fella. Two other varsity letterman returning from last year's squad were Larry Park and Mac Green. Also on the team were, Barry Ebersol, Mike O'Neil (transfer from Maine), Tim Northern, Billy Wilson, Charles Reno, Louis Zamudio, Gary Hahs, and Kenneth Lester (a transfer from

Georgia). The team wasn't too tall this year, no one on this squad was taller than Scoggin. Perhaps if they had been taller they would have made it deeper into the playoffs. They didn't dissatisfy their coach though, Butler called these guys, "the best little team I ever had."

The 1966-67 season had many highs and lows. There were untimely injuries, unusual distractions and unfortunate illnesses throughout the year. One of their lowest moments was a loss at home to Barstow, an even littler team led by five foot seven inch point guard, Glenn Massengale (who later became principal at VVHS and Butler's boss). Butler thought his boys could handle the smaller, quicker Riffians (that was their mascot then— something like a Sultan) man-to-man. They couldn't. Barstow was just too quick. Massengale ran circles around Steve Scoggin who had previously assured Butler he could stop him. Stubbornly, Butler wouldn't switch to a zone defense even though it was obvious to everyone they needed to get out of the man defense. "We lost 77-72 and it was my fault," Butler said. "We never should have played them man-to-man in the first place."

But one of Victor Valley's high points in the season came in the rematch against Barstow in their gym. "We played zone and beat them by 34," Butler recalled proudly.

When Mac Green and Steve Scoggin were too sick to play at Burroughs, Victor dropped a game they needed to win in order to be assured a playoff berth. This loss put the ultimate pressure on them. Now they had to win their last game of the season on the road if they were going to make it into post season play. And who were they playing? The first place team of course.

I wish I could give you a story-book ending but the reality is the Jackrabbits lost and missed the playoffs though the loss was a 74-72 thriller. Mac Green was almost a hero. With the score tied 72-72, he stole the ball from an Antelope Valley player with less than 20 seconds left in the game and took it the length of the court to score, putting VVHS up 74-72, before a late whistle reversed the situation. Instead, Green was called for a reaching-in foul which gave the Antelopes a one-and-one free throw opportunity, which they cashed in on by sinking them both. Instead, Antelope Valley won 74-72 when the Rabbits missed a last second shot to tie.

In Butler's view, the officials were out of position to make the call on Green. From where Butler sat he saw a clean steal. Needless to say, he was irate about the call. It felt like a homer job. He chewed on the officials for a while. It wouldn't be the last time Butler disagreed with officials.

With a 17-8 finish, Butler had accumulated a five year record of 88-27. He was a proven winner. His newest star, Jerry Hyder, was set to follow Greg to Eastern New Mexico and he might even have the right stuff to play pro ball (he did, he was drafted by the Denver Rockets of the ABA). In an end of the season interview with the local paper, Butler called Jerry Hyder, "the best player I've ever had." By season's end, Jerry Hyder led the Rabbits in 15 statistical categories. But Butler didn't just work with the stars. Mac Green and Larry Park had developed well enough to go on to play community college basketball while Steve Scoggin had earned a scholarship to Whittier College.

In 1967-68, Butler got a whiff of something that smelled bad, his first losing season as a varsity coach. Victor Valley was the preseason favorite to win the league title until four key players moved away before school started. VVHS was frequently impacted by George Air Force Base, just five miles north of Victorville. It was always a crapshoot with kids from the base. Some years Butler got great transfers in. Other years great players transferred out. This year Butler lost a lot of talent due to transfers out.

Left with only Al Brolsma and Gary Hahs to carry the load—then Hahs came down with mononucleosis and missed a month—Butler had to forage through the C and B teams to find suitable replacements. Fortunately, he found a diamond in the rough in sophomore Paul Hernandez, who to this day still shares the single game high scoring record at VVHS. (Hernandez broke Norman Olsen's three day old scoring record of 43 points by scoring 44, and that was back before the three point shot. Jason Bragg tied him in Butler's last season, 1989-90, but Jason did it mostly on three-pointers.)

Victor Valley's preseason favorite status evaporated quickly as they opened up 1-10 in December. Butler had never felt anything like this before. It ran a close second to the sick feeling he got when the University of Oklahoma told him he couldn't play ball any more because of his tachycardia.

League play didn't do much to turn things around either. The Jackrabbits stumbled through a 3-9 season to finish 4-19 for the year. Butler, however, refused to dwell on the negatives. When VVHS lost a hard fought season finale 65-70 to perennial contender Antelope Valley, Butler told sportswriter Jim Duncan, "I wish the season were starting over again. We were beginning to play some fine ball near the end."

In 28 years at VVHS, Butler had only three losing seasons, yet Butler loved the boys on his losing teams just as much as he did those on his winners. He seldom failed to praise his players' efforts in those losing seasons, stressing their dedication, hustle, determination and improvement. "I'm just as proud of these boys playing for me this year as any I've ever had," Butler said in the final newspaper article of the 1967-68 season.

The problem with a losing season is that sometimes losing generates more losing. This can be devastating for a coach who questions his own

71

philosophy. What am I doing wrong? What should I change? Am I playing the right combination of players? Did I cut the wrong players? Etcetera. Fortunately, Butler didn't start questioning his philosophy after one losing season. He chalked it up to losing four of his best players to transfers. He'd learned way back at St. Joseph's that in order to win consistently you had to have talent. Last year he didn't have much.

The 1968-69 team was slightly more experienced and a bit more talented. They were led by junior Paul Hernandez and senior Norman Olson. Again Butler brought up some sophomores, two of whom had been an incredible scoring tandem for Danny Ribbons' ninth grade team at Victor Junior the past season: Louie Zamudio and Gayland Park—dubbed the "Super Sophs." Butler didn't like to bring up sophomores. He'd only brought up three so far in his years at VVHS, but Butler was desperate to get back on the winning track after his first losing season and he believed sophomores Zamudio and Park could help offensively. The rest of the roster included: Ron Miffin, Roy Brechlin, Dickie Johnson, Sal Hinojos, Al Hom, Robert Tedford and Manuel Villegas. Of the entire roster, 10 had no varsity experience, and their center, Brechlin, was only six foot two inches tall.

The team doubled last year's number of wins plus one, going 9-13. They were a mediocre 4-5 in pre-league play and 5-8 in league games. There were no playoffs for the third year in a row, few accolades and a bit of a letdown in the community that had grown to expect so much from Butler's teams. However, there were some strong boys who would be moving up off the championship C team—namely Armando Quinones and Tex Navarro—who would help catapult VVHS back into Golden League title contention next season.

VVHS 1970-74

The 1970s began on a high note for Butler. Three year varsity letterman and All Golden League player, Paul Hernandez, six foot seven inch sophomore, Steve Lantz, Louie Zamudio, Gay Park, Armando Quinones, Tex Navarro, Al Hom, Roy Brechlin, Terry Lee, Dickie Johnson, Frank Minor and Pat Gatchell all combined to bring home Butler's third league title in eight years. This team set a school record of 12 wins in a row, went 12-2 in league, and finished the season 18-6. Their only real low point was a first round CIF playoff loss, 45-48 to Riverside North. Other than that, they'd had a hugely successful year and Butler couldn't have been more satisfied after back to back losing seasons. Best of all, Butler had a high scoring cadre of juniors returning in 1970-71 to help him close in on his 200th career coaching win.

The 1970-71 squad was heavily laden with experienced seniors; they also had four big scoring dynamos in: Armando Quinones, Tex Navarro, Gayland Park, and "court magician" Louie Zamudio. These four rarely combined for less than 60 points per game. The rest of the team consisted of: Robert Sherwood, Rick Lawyer, Dan Dawson, Mark Staggs, Eddie Villegas, Geoff Carter and Bill Maier. Yet, with all their experience and high-powered offense, these guys only managed to get off to an average start.

By the end of pre-league play in December they were 5-7; however, Butler wasn't worried. He had taken it upon himself in the Sixties to get out of scheduling contracts with the small schools VVHS always played in pre-league prior to him taking over. Now the Rabbits had bigger schools scheduled in their stead. By the time the Seventies rolled around there were no more easy pre-league wins to pick up, every victory had to be earned. The Rabbits competed in both the Laguna Beach and Newport Harbor tournaments this year, and though they lost to big schools with quality teams in close games, Butler was happy with the team's effort and felt they were well prepared for league play even though their record was under .500.

The first Golden League game was auspicious and boded a positive momentum shift. At Antelope Valley, Armando Quinones hit a jumper from the corner with one second to go to break a 69-69 tie and win it for the Rabbits. But Quinones wasn't the true hero of the game, that honor went to Gayland Park, who finished with 26 points and earned both of Butler's coveted offensive and defensive "Player of the Game" awards.

To motivate his players, Butler kept detailed statistics. He had an army of stat girls keeping track of everything from missed shots to loose ball recoveries. After each game he would tally the stats once he got home, then select both an offensive and defensive Player of the Game which he would give a certificate to at the next practice. These selections were based on the overall plus / minus points a player earned in the game. I won't get into all the details of how this stat process worked, except to say that Butler used it motivationally and his players enjoyed the recognition he gave.

Armando Quinones won the offensive award next game though when he pumped in 26 points to lead the Rabbits—who used a smothering full-court press—past the Burros 71-59. It wasn't too long into league play before Butler began touting Quinones as "probably the best pure shooter I've ever had." And he was a great shooter, I remember that, even though I was only in the eighth grade at the time. That was when I first started going to the high school games. Armando was a lanky six foot three and didn't look all that athletic—especially with his Mickey Dolenz of the Monkees haircut, but when he'd pull up for his patented baseline jumper from 20 feet his form was perfect and he almost always swished the shot.

The Victor Valley Jackrabbits provided a much needed distraction about this time. The Charles Manson trial and the Vietnam War dominated the front pages of the local paper with news of murder and mayhem, both legal and criminal; fortunately, more positive news could be found on the sports page. The Jackrabbits were playing some stellar ball. Though they finished 10-4 in league, their four losses were all games they could just as easily have won. Three of the losses were by two points each, the fourth loss by nine—on a night when the entire offense sputtered and only one player reached double-figures. On second thought, maybe they couldn't have won that one. As always, Butler stayed positive after each of the losses.

A coach's job is to motivate the players to recover from a loss not berate them for losing. Butler seldom berated his players. To show you another of his positive ways of handling losing, here's what Butler had to say after a tough overtime loss to Burros, "I can't fault the players, they gave it everything they had. They gave more than 100 percent, if that's possible."

Unfortunately, the season ended on a sour note, as seasons always do if you don't go to the title game and win it. VVHS drew Los Altos, the number two seed, in the first round of the CIF playoffs. Though Victor Valley thoroughly out played Los Altos, according to Butler, foul trouble and missed free-throws were the two reasons they lost 59-65. While the underclassmen could look forward to redeeming themselves next year, the seniors had to draw the curtain on their high school basketball careers. They finished 14-11 overall.

Butler had to rebuild the Jackrabbits in 1971-72. All the scoring last season had come from the seniors so returning lettermen Bill Maier, Robert Sherwood, Geoff Carter and Rick Lawyer would be relied on heavily this season to pick up where last year's seniors left off. Joining the four returners were Jeff Armstrong, Aaron Thomas, Jerry Ronnebeck, Darrel Hagen, Kevin Long, Ruben Hernandez and Rod Toner. The best players on this squad, Butler figured, were going to be Bill Maier and Rick Lawyer—based on what they did last year as back-ups.

In pre-league play the Rabbits did about the same as they had the previous year, going 4-5 in December against the big-city schools; but unlike last year's team, they couldn't get any momentum going during league play. They went an even 7-7, to finish 11-12 overall, giving Butler his third, and last, losing season of his 35 year coaching career. However, the 1971-72 squad had its memorable moments. Against the Burros of Ridgecrest they burned the nets for 107 points to set a school game high scoring record.

In 1972-73, the Jackrabbits returned four varsity athletes who had gained valuable experience on a competitive though inconsistent 1971-72 squad. This year those four: Jerry Ronnebeck, Neiland McCloney, Darrel Hagen and Jeff Armstrong would lead the Jackrabbits to a much better record. They were joined by newcomers: Jack Borja, Terry Tobin, David Alonzo, Henry Alvarado, Dennis Lopez and Dexter Caffee.

This is the era when I played and am I ever tempted to tell you off-color stories about practically any one of these guys. Some of them I went to Catholic school with, others I knew from Boy Scouts, and still others I knew from the community plunge or the bowling alley or Little League baseball. Victorville was a small town. You knew everybody. But they might get mad at me if I reveal any of their less flattering moments, so rather than digress into the six degrees of separation between members of a small town, I'll resist the temptation to delve into side-bars and only mention one basketball related story before returning to the main plot.

As sophomores in Butler's program our C team was hugely successful under Butler's Irish assistant, the leprechaun Joe Shea—even though our season began with a loss. In our first high school game ever, we fell to Mater Dei, 70-72, in overtime at their place, on a blatantly bad call by an obviously biased home-town official, probably a dad of one of their players. It was a loss but being robbed the way we were we didn't feel like losers. We then went on to win fifteen games in a row before we lost our only other game of the season, 50-51 to Palmdale, on a last second shot. (We would have won if Joe Campbell hadn't missed a two foot lay-up by 20 feet with seconds to go.) We finished the season 20-2 and figured the class of '75 was pretty hot stuff.

About midway through the season we must have been making some pretty offensive noise about how our team was the best team in the program and Butler got wind of it. He knew just what to do to take the arrogance out of our sails, Butler made our team scrimmage the varsity. He picked the perfect time for it, too.

The varsity had just come off an upset loss and they were not happy about it. They got madder when Butler told them our boast of being the best team in the program. We were in a very tight place. It was too late to take back what we'd said. Butler told us to come in for a scrimmage against his team to settle who was the best team in the program.

Instead of coming in to practice at our usual 4-6 p.m. time slot, we came in at 2:45. The varsity had already practiced for 45 minutes and were warmed up and waiting for us. When Joe Shea let us into the gym the varsity disappeared into the locker room while we went through our lay-up drills. I imagine Butler gave them a little last minute instruction about how he wanted them to handle us—the bragging little brothers in the program.

We were in the neighborhood of a 13-1 record about that time and knew we were a good team. We hit the open man like nobody's business. Our team was very unselfish. We had height, quickness, great shooters and so much talent that Butler agreed with Joe Shea that he didn't see how he could trim the roster below 20 guys. Our first 15 guys could have started for most any other school. We rolled over teams. In our league opener we beat Apple Valley 80-20. Winning brought confidence. Confidence bred cockiness. Against other sophomore teams we were a force to be reckoned with, but boneheads that we were at 15 years of age, we thought that meant we could compete with 17 and 18 year olds. We were about to get a reality check.

Butler lined us up just like it was a real game. He had junior varsity coaches, Willie McDonald and Steve Scoggin, officiate. We got virtually no calls from them and much to our surprise our own coach never argued on our behalf. From the first quarter opening tip to the end of the fourth quarter horn the varsity showed no mercy. Hagen and Ronnebeck, big muscular guys, knocked us around so bad we were afraid to come into the paint. Neiland McCloney shocked us with Ebonics we'd never heard. Armstrong, Alvarado, and Caffee intimidated us with trash talk about us being insignificant scrubby sophomores punks. We were constantly picking ourselves up off the floor right and left, with nary a whistle sounding. By the second quarter we were scared to death of those guys and by the end of the fourth quarter our comeuppance was so complete that we instinctively knew shooting off our mouths about how good we were was no longer an option. We couldn't compete with the varsity. They were men. We were boys. It was a lesson I'll never forget.

The 1972-73 Jackrabbits could have easily won the league instead of coming in second like they did. They went 7-3 in pre-league play and Jeff Armstrong emerged as the team's leading scorer. He was named All-Tournament at the San Bernardino Kiwanis Tournament and was the tournament's leading scorer in averaging 25 points per game.

When league play began in January it looked like the Rabbits would run away from the rest of the league as they ran off four straight wins. At 4-0 in league and 11-3 overall most coaches would be pretty happy with a team's momentum, but Butler saw signs of overconfidence setting in and he referred to it in an interview with a local sportswriter following a victorious but lackluster performance against Kennedy. "Our players," he noted, "have been resting on their laurels. They must realize when you're good there is always somebody ready to get you, and this team better be prepared." Butler, the master psychologist, often used his responses to sportswriter's questions to motivate his players. His comments were calculated subliminal challenges. Usually they achieved the desired long-term affect, this time they only worked temporarily.

In their next outing the Jackrabbits trounced Antelope Valley 72-47 to show their coach there was no laurel resting. At 12-3 they had proven they were good and felt they had every right to be confident. Butler needn't be concerned about them letting up and getting upset, but that turned out to be the pride coming before the fall, a fall that proved Butler an unheeded prophet.

The Burros of Ridgecrest were happy to play spoiler and give the Jackrabbits their due. They were just one game back of VVHS in the standings at 4-1. Short story to be told, late in the game frustration set in and a technical foul against a Victor Valley player (did I mention Darrel Hagen's temper) turned a tie game into a five point deficit for the Rabbits which they couldn't overcome, losing 76-73 at home and snapping an eight game winning streak. They were now 5-1 and tied with Ridgecrest for first place. Butler shook his head, but in a way he was as glad as a coach can be in defeat; he knew his team needed this loss as a healthy dose of medicine to cure their overconfidence.

The medicine worked well. The Jackrabbits won their next four league games and earned back sole possession of first place at 9-1; unfortunately, they didn't hold onto their lead for long. They were upset by Kennedy 70-62. Butler said, "The loss didn't mark our funeral," but he was worried about what the loss would do to their momentum. With three games to go they still had to face Antelope Valley and Ridgecrest again, two teams which regularly played VVHS tough. You didn't want to start losing just as the playoffs were coming up.

VVHS beat Antelope Valley next and everyone breathed a sigh of relief. They were 10-2 and again tied with the Burros of Ridgecrest for first, which set up a great high school showdown for the league crown in the Burros' "snakepit," as Butler sneeringly refers to their gym. But come game time VVHS was in trouble, Butler's team was reeling with the flu. Back-up guard, Jerry Hernandez, and center, Neiland McCloney, didn't make the trip, while Jeff Armstrong, Darrel Hagen and Jerry Ronnebeck were all sick, too, but not sick enough to be bed-ridden. Courageously, they played, but the Rabbits fell 66-64, giving Burros a one game lead with one game to go.

Both VVHS and Ridgecrest won their last game, giving Victor Valley a second place finish with an 11-3 record. This meant they would draw a tougher opponent in first round and play their first playoff game on the road. When the seedings came out, sure enough, VVHS had drawn a tough first round opponent. They would face the number one seed, the 28-1 Garey High School Vikings of Pomona, one of the most highly regarded high school teams in the entire country.

The Vikings were led by future NBA forward, six foot eight inch, Greg Ballard, and six foot ten inch center, Tim LaMaster. While Butler was hopeful that the Jackrabbits could compete with Garey, realistically he knew it would take a near perfect game to upset them. That perfect game did not materialize, though it did produce a humorous anecdote that came out at the Class of '75 reunion years later.

Flash forward 27 years to the Class of 1975's 25th reunion at Avalon Park in Victorville. It's October 20, 2000. We are reminiscing about the old days and somehow the topic of the playoff game against Garey when we were sophomores comes up.

Steve Williams, an incredible leaper on our 20-2 sophomore team, recounted the story about how he watched Greg Ballard from the end of the bench. At six foot three, Williams led our sophomore team in rebounds. He was one of those rare white men that could jump. When the CIF playoffs rolled around, Butler brought up four of the five starters on our C team to get some experience, since he was planning on all four of those guys playing varsity the following year as juniors. They were: Bill Roes, Oscar Lugo, Steve Sawaia and Steve Williams. The rest of us sophomores who didn't get moved up to the varsity rode down to the playoff game in the rooter's bus so we could raucously cheer our sophomore teammates on, knowing the only action they would get would be in the pre-game warm-ups.

Williams, who knew that many major college scouts would be there watching Ballard and LaMaster, did his best to wow some of the recruiters into noticing him as he performed acrobatic dunks every time he went in for a lay-up in warm-ups. To help him get added attention, we bellowed out loud cheers from the stands every time he dunked and pretty soon there were a number of people saying, "Hey, check out the long-haired hippie, that boy can get up!" But when the pre-game warm-ups ended, Williams knew he was done for the night.

When the game started, the Garey Vikings raced out to an early first quarter 20 point lead that they never relinquished, and though VVHS held Ballard to a mere 28 points and 26 rebounds (no sarcasm here, that was good effort against Ballard who regularly scored over 40 points a game and often grabbed as many rebounds), they were never able to get back into the game in the second half, losing 85-63. We were way overmatched.

Williams, who had an unobstructed view of Ballard throughout the game from his front row seat at the end of the Victor Valley bench, was awe-struck at the way Ballard dominated his own team's big men. He was glad he was only a sophomore and wouldn't have to go up against him. But early in the fourth quarter, Butler began looking down the bench for replacements. Even though Butler was a never-say-die coach, it was apparent that the Jackrabbits weren't going to pull off a miracle. The whole game they were behind, sometimes as far back as 30 points. The starters were having little success against the much bigger and stronger Vikings. Butler thought it might be a good time to get his younger players some playoff experience. Maybe they could even get a little rally going.

When Williams saw Butler looking down the bench, he leaned waaaay back to obscure himself behind the other 13 players seated in a long line of folding chairs. He was lucky to have a good seat far away from Butler and his assistant coaches. Williams didn't want to go in until Garey had taken Ballard out. Silently, Williams began praying, "Don't put me in Coach, don't put me in." At 15 years old and 165 pounds, Williams wanted no part of the 18 year old, 250 pound man-child, Greg Ballard, who would become the Washington Bullets number one draft pick out of Oregon St. in 1977. When Butler pointed to Dennis Lopez and Bill Roes to go in, Williams breathed a huge sigh of relief. "There is a God! Thank you!"

Although the 1972-73 Jackrabbits finished second in league and were eliminated from the playoffs in the first round, they still had a terrific year. They ended up 18-7. Three seniors played college basketball off that team, and one of those players, Jeff Armstrong, went all the way to the big show.

Of all Butler's players who went on to play college ball, Jeff Armstrong had one of the longest careers as a player and coach. After a couple years playing at the community college level, Armstrong picked up a scholarship to play for Point Loma College in San Diego; then, after he graduated, he landed a basketball player's dream job as a member of the California Chiefs and the Washington Generals, teams that traveled with the Harlem

79

Globetrotters (up until the New York Nationals took over in 1995). Armstrong, one of Victor Valley's best shooting guards, spent a number of years (from 1977-81) helping the Globetrotters put on fabulous shows around the world. After that he coached five years in Saudi Arabia. Currently, he is teaching and coaching in the San Diego area. He says that although he and Butler conflicted during his senior year, he has long since come to understand what Butler was trying to teach him then and now he patterns his own personal life and coaching philosophy after Butler's. Armstrong cites Butler as being "after my father, the most influential man in my life, and I played for lots of different coaches."

Perhaps Ollie Butler's showmanship rubbed off on Armstrong, too. In fact, it was just before Armstrong graduated from high school that Butler put on one of his best performances. On June 1, 1973, Butler showed up at school dancing, jiving, joking and merrymaking like never before. Who was this jolly Ollie? What was animating him?

Butler had long ago laid to rest the dream of having a son who would grow up to play basketball for him. Sharon had given him three lovely daughters and they were all Daddies' girls. He loved them deeply and was in no way discontent at not having a male scion. In the early Seventies, with the girls all in Catholic school, Sharon had returned to college at Cal State San Bernardino to finish her undergraduate degree in history. She planned on going into elementary education. The last thing Sharon planned on was having another baby. Their youngest, Cathy, was almost nine, Becky was eleven and Jana was a new teenager. However, the Catholic "rhythm method" of birth control wasn't an exact science, and God, with his clever sense of humor, has a way of surprising even the best family planners. In October of 1972, Sharon broke the news to Ollie that she was pregnant. Ollie was thrilled. He couldn't lose. Perhaps he might get his son after all, though if he didn't he'd be just as happy with another daughter. Throughout the entire 1972-73 season, Butler's mind would occasionally stray off during a game and he would speculate what it would be like to have a son playing for him who shot the lights out of the gym the way Jeff Armstrong did.

Amniocentesis—the test to determine a child's sex before birth—was not yet the common procedure it is today so the Butler's had to wait it out the old fashioned way. That's why Butler was so ecstatic when he came by school after his son was born, he was still riding the crescent wave of wonder at the birth of Michael Kevin Butler. The faculty, staff and students were surprised at the normally calm, cool and collected Butler. Everyone knew that only basketball got Butler emotional, off the court he was always the low key, polite, Southern gentleman. Yet here he was gamboling around like a kid at an amusement park. "It's a boy! It's a boy!" It looked like

Butler was going to have a son grow up and play for him after all. He started counting the years.

The war in Vietnam and the election scandal known as Watergate were on the minds of the American people as Butler opened his eleventh year teaching and coaching at VVHS. Popular social studies teacher that he was, Butler continued to revel in the current events of the day, knowing that a pageant of history was unfolding in the morning papers, weekly news magazines and on the nightly news broadcasts. As much as he loved the athletic outlet of coaching basketball, he equally enjoyed the intellectual aspect of teaching history, and with a world so topsy-turvy, teaching American history seemed like the easiest thing in the world to be doing.

The 16 and 17 year old students Butler had as American history students wanted to know about their world. They were in no way resistant to learning, rather, they were genuinely interested in why times were so tumultuous. Going into the past to show how former events set the stage for current situations, Butler was revered by his students as an interesting teacher who made history relevant to what was going on currently in the world. But when the last bell rang each day, Butler went through a Clark Kent type transformation.

Walking down the corridors of Victor Valley High, Butler looked to anyone like an ordinary, bookish, history teacher, yet upon emerging from the locker room to open the gym, he became Super coach: athletic, wiry, trim, energetic, competitive, prepared and driven.

Butler told me once that, "While I dearly loved teaching history, I looked so forward to the last bell of the day so I could change into my shorts and sneakers, sweep down the gym floor and begin warming up with some free-shooting with the players." The truth of the matter is that Butler got into coaching because he wanted to keep playing basketball the rest of his life. When the coaching staff at Oklahoma told him he couldn't play for them anymore because of what the doctors said about his tachycardia, it didn't take Butler long to figure out that as a coach he could still play, yet not have to put himself through the extreme physical exertion that his players would have to go through to get into top shape to play 32 minutes a game for 20-30 games in a season.

Steve Scoggins, who had returned to Victor Valley as a social studies teacher and coach to begin the 1972-73 season, following a successful four years playing basketball at Whittier College, was now Butler's junior varsity coach. He was in his second year now and he was my coach this season. He was a Butler protégé, having known Butler since the seventh grade at Hook Junior High in 1961-62, Butler's first year in Victorville.

When I called Steve to interview him, he was even more enthused than many of Butler's other former players I talked to. Butler had influenced his life so much, he was glad to hear someone was writing a book about him. (That's the universal comment I got from most everyone when I told them about this project.) I already told you a little about how impressed Steve was with Butler on the baseball field. Steve said Butler made an equal impression on him as a kid in his science class. "The one thing I will never forget is that he told us never to put anything in our ear smaller than a football. I sat there wondering for the life of me, how could you put a football in your ear." Steve and his older brother Fella took to Butler immediately. They both played football, basketball and track for Butler at Hook, Steve on the seventh grade teams in 1961-62, and Fella on the ninth grade teams.

When Butler moved up to Victor Valley to take over the basketball program after a year at Hook, Fella Scoggin made the varsity as a sophomore. Steve, then in the eighth grade, would catch the bus to VVHS after school where their mom would pick him and his brother up after Fella's practice was over. Steve remembers playing Butler one-on-one nearly everyday while Fella was showering after practice. "Butler never let me win either. He was merciless. I remember him saying one time, 'I think that's 45 wins to none.'" In retrospect, Steve realized that Butler was only helping him to become a better player. "If he'd have eased up on me, I wouldn't have developed my same level of competitiveness. I wanted to win so bad because of all those losses he dealt me."

When Steve finally got to high school, his brother was a senior on the varsity. He didn't figure Butler was going to have time to play one-on-one with him any more. Things couldn't have turned out more differently. Butler lost his sophomore coach so he took over that team too. Scoggin was glad because this meant he would get to play Butler one- on-one again, either before or after practice. Amazingly, Butler, at the same time he coached the varsity to a 20-3 record, coached Steve Scoggin's sophomore team to a 19-0 finish. And again, he beat Steve every time they played one-on-one.

When Scoggin returned in 1972 as Butler's assistant coach they resumed their afternoon ritual and I remember watching them go at it a few times. Now it was Scoggin, in his prime at about 23 or 24 years old, who regularly beat Butler, although Butler at 43 could still manage to pull out a win every so often. But Scoggin and Butler together against any two varsity or junior varsity players were tremendous, those guys were the masters of two-on-two. We never beat them. They pick and rolled us to death, and rarely did either ever miss an open jump shot. Scoggin had learned to shoot from Butler way back when, and together they were an unstoppable tandem.

The one thing Steve wanted to make sure I got across was that Butler was a competitive athlete whose love for the game was infectious. Steve had the same high praise for Butler that Jimmy Dickerson did. "Butler was a tremendous role model," Steve said. "I wanted to teach history and coach basketball because I wanted to be just like Ollie Butler. If I hadn't have met him, I wouldn't have the great life I have now."

By the time the 1973-74 season began, Butler had long since developed the knack for balancing his varsity squad. He always had a core group of experienced seniors who were returning lettermen, a handful of four or five juniors who would see action and gain experience, and maybe a sophomore or two if they were especially promising. On the varsity level to kick off the 1973-74 season, Butler had four varsity returners: Henry "the Hawk" Alvarado, Jerry Hernandez, Dexter "Defense" Caffee and Dennis Lopez. Up from the JV team he had promoted: Leon Edwards, Roy Neighbors, Mike Schuerich and Mike Mulcahy, and off our 20-2 sophomore team he took: Steve Sawaia, Bill Roes, Steve Williams and Oscar Lugo. As an added bonus, Butler pilfered a rangy six foot three inch incoming sophomore, Clifford Boyd, from Joe Shea's C team. This team would kick off the start of a ten year run of consecutive league championships. Ollie Butler was entering the heyday of his career.

In the annual Christmas Kiwanis Tournament in San Bernardino, VVHS won three of four games and finished the pre-league month of December with a mediocre 4-6 record. Going into Kiwanis their record was 1-5 but in the tournament they turned things around and won some close games instead of losing them. Butler wasn't down on his squad though, all six losses had come by a combined average of three points per loss and the losses had been against bigger schools with traditionally strong basketball programs.

To Butler, this was what the pre-league games were all about. Each year he took a new group of guys and taught them how to fight through adversity, how to overcome the odds, how to develop character and how to compete with bigger, stronger, more athletic opponents. Basically the same stuff you need to know to be successful in life. Butler felt this always prepared his teams for league play against schools of equal size. Also, throughout the pre-league month of December, Butler strove to instill something he learned from Long Beach State coach, Jerry Tarkanian, that if you can get your boys to play harder than the opponent, you can usually pick up six extra wins a season against teams that might be better than you but just don't work like you do.

League play started off with an exciting 53-51 defeat of cross town rival Apple Valley. Butler had dominated Apple Valley since they joined the Golden League in 1968. In 13 games his Jackrabbits had won 12 of them.

Next VVHS rolled over Palmdale, Kennedy and Antelope Valley before losing to Burros, now under the guidance of a former Butler assistant, Larry Bird, whom Steve Scoggin replaced. Bird didn't waste any time in beating his former mentor 75-67.

Their first league loss after four straight wins sent VVHS into a tailspin. They lost their next two games, to Barstow in overtime 58-59, and to Quartz Hill 54-60, where Butler swore the officials homered the Rabbits in their own gym. "I will be pleased to be on the road Friday," Butler chortled to the *Daily Press* sports reporter after the Quartz Hill loss. "Maybe on a foreign court we'll get a better job from the officials. Most teams in basketball have a home court advantage. We don't!"

Which brings us face to face with the dilemma that plagued Butler throughout his career, the problem he had with officials. Butler wants to make it clear he always accepted that there were less talented and more talented officials, just like there were less talented and more talented athletes. As a frustrated perfectionist he could deal with that, but what Butler had little patience for was incompetence. And as you will see in the seasons to come, Butler's relationship with officials became an axis around which controversy revolved. The more knowledgeable he became as a basketball coach, the more incompetent officials seemed to become.

Butler's wish for better officiating was granted on the road against Palmdale. Butler praised the referees after VVHS escaped with a 48-45 win over the Falcons. This was followed by the opening game of their second round of league, a rematch with Apple Valley, in which Butler saw his team play their best game of the year. "That was the best defense I've seen in my entire coaching career," Butler shouted jubilantly to his players in the locker room after the win.

Victor Valley followed with a thrashing of Kennedy and seemed to be peaking until Antelope Valley upset them 63-61; but having learned from Butler how to handle adverse situations, the Rabbits bounced back and won all three of their remaining league games.

The Rabbits avenged their loss to Burros by using "Dexter Defense" on Burros' scoring ace Steve Nathan. Dexter Caffee was Butler's best defensive player. He was a lightning quick, lean, energetic, angular, six foot one inch defensive phenomenon. He was well known throughout the league as a prime defensive commodity. If an opponent had an unstoppable scorer, Butler sent Caffee out to guard him. He had guarded some of the best scorers in Southern California in his two years on the varsity. Dexter Defense always prevailed, at least until he fouled out. Against Burros, Butler used a box-and-one, which coaches know as a four man zone defense in the form of a box and one man playing man-for-man defense, in this case Dexter Caffee on Nathan, shadowing him wherever he went. It worked so well that Butler used it again successfully in their next game against Barstow. While Dexter's defense was a significant factor in the win over Barstow, he wasn't the only game hero. Junior, Bill Roes, drilled two free throws with seconds left on the clock to lift VVHS to a 56-55 win. That momentum propelled Victor Valley through their final Golden League game, a 70-59 victory over Quartz Hill, giving them a 10-4 record and earning them a tie for the league title with the 10-4 Burros.

Victor Valley again went to the CIF playoffs. This was Butler's seventh trip in twelve years. In the first round they knocked off a competitive Yucaipa team 60-58 in overtime. Junior, Steve Williams, contributed greatly to that win by coming off the bench in the second half to pull down nine rebounds. In the second round though, the shots didn't fall for the Rabbits in a home game against Brawley. In a cold-shooting game for both teams, the score was a mere 16-15 at halftime and it didn't get any better in the second half. Winter would not let go and the Jackrabbits stayed frigid all night. In the end, they lost by two. Had a missed goaltending call, that everyone in the gym seemed to see except the officials (more incompetence), given the Rabbits the two points they deserved, they could just as easily have won. The final score was a VVHS playoff record low 31-33.

And on a side-note, perhaps if back-up guard Steve Sawaia, son of then head Jackrabbit football coach Wade Sawaia, hadn't quit the day before the second round game to join the baseball team, perhaps he could have given them the additional three points they needed to win. On our 20-2 sophomore team Steve was the leading scorer, averaging over 20 points per game. Yet, as a junior, playing behind seniors Jerry Hernandez, Dexter Caffee, and Henry Alvarado, Steve had only played sparing minutes. Ever since the sixth grade Steve had been a starter and the leading scorer on every basketball team he played on and it was hard for him to sit on the bench most of his junior year waiting for Butler to call on him. Plus there was the rift between Butler and his father. Steve wondered if that had anything to do with his lack of playing time. Numerous times he'd complained to Butler that he thought he should be playing more. It never helped.

Baseball pre-season began the same time VVHS entered the basketball playoffs. Steve, who had started at catcher on the varsity as a sophomore, was itching to get back behind the plate. He knew that on the baseball team he'd be playing, not sitting and watching, and not only that, the baseball team had a pre-season tournament coming up that Sawaia wanted to play in. If the basketball team kept winning in the playoffs Sawaia would miss that tournament so just before the Brawley game he decided to call it a career on the hardwood and quit the team.

I was disappointed when Sawaia quit. I tried to talk him out of it. We'd gone to school together since the first grade. We lived across the street from each other and had played all sports together since we could first pick up a ball. I was looking forward to playing again with Steve next year on the varsity. We were great teammates because we knew each other's moves so well, but this year, for the first time ever, we had been on different teams, him on the varsity and me on the JVs. I was sure that we would have a fantastic year on the varsity together as seniors, yet here he was hanging up basketball. Ouch! But as a friend I could understand his discouragement. You're on a basketball team that apparently doesn't need you since you aren't getting much playing time. You aren't getting along with the coach, who you think has a grudge against you. But there's a baseball team that wants you badly. All you want to do is play. You're tired of being a spectator, sitting and watching. I guess I might have quit too if I'd have been in Steve's shoes.

Without Steve Sawaia, Butler's Jackrabbits finished 15-11 overall. Standing at mid-court while talking to the press after the Brawley loss, Butler said of all the teams he'd had in his nearly 20 years of coaching, "This is the most courageous group of players I've had. We had no extraordinary talent, but they made up for it with effort. It's all over with, but it doesn't leave a bitter taste. We had a fine season for an undermanned bunch of fellows." And as a tribute to Butler's coaching, five of those undermanned fellows went on to play college ball at one level or another in the fall.

VVHS: THE 1975 SEASON

My senior year in high school is memorable for many reasons but none more so than playing varsity basketball for Ollie Butler. Our football team went 0-9. For this we were razzed by our own classmates and called "losers." Ollie Butler brought redemption. We went from losers to winners. Under his guidance our basketball team went 22-5 (which oddly enough is the same record Ollie Butler had his senior year in high school on the basketball team, not that I believe in numerology or anything).

Our team was talented and as a group we had a long tradition of winning going back to successive league titles at the junior high. The guys who played for Danny Ribbons had won the league every year since the 7th grade, losing maybe one or two games at most each season. The rest of our team came from Hook Junior, except for one military transfer, and the teams at Hook were used to winning too. (They always took second place to Victor Junior.) When you have a tradition of winning it breeds confidence. Under Butler at VVHS the winning continued.

Unlike some teams that have a drop off in skilled players after the sixth or seventh man, we didn't. Our second string regularly challenged the first string, often beating them in practice scrimmages, and there wasn't much of a drop off in talent between our very best player and the last man on the roster. In fact, at midpoint during league play, *Daily Press* sportswriter Ernie Castillo called our second string "the second best team in the Golden League." It's no wonder our team was so sound, we only had three underclassmen.

Our lone sophomore was Tony Anderson, who many acclaim as the finest basketball player ever to come out of Victor Valley High. Anyone who knows anything about Victor Valley basketball knows the now legendary name of Tony Anderson. He demolished all the school's previous rebounding and scoring records in his career at VVHS and when he graduated in 1977 he was named the CIF 2A Player of the Year. No one at VVHS before or since has received the accolades that Tony Anderson earned. But as a sophomore on the varsity, Tony was just a pup. He didn't start for us, rather, he backed up our three big men; but there were many times when it seemed like Tony started so quickly was he inserted into the game. I remember our center, Bill Roes, drawing a foul just after the tip-off in one game. Hooooonk went the horn! With seven seconds ticked off the first quarter clock Anderson was inserted into the game and out came Roes to sit next to Butler and have an index finger waggled in his face and his ear filled with a harangue on stupid fouls in the early going.

The other two underclassmen on our team were juniors: Clifford Boyd and Sergio Lugo. Boyd played on the varsity as a sophomore and eventually became a starter in his rookie season. He was six foot three inches tall and had a knack for positioning himself to get rebounds. He was also a pretty good scorer in the paint. In his three years at VVHS he broke all of Greg Hyder's old rebounding records. Unfortunately for Boyd, Tony Anderson came along right behind him to erase them and have his own name written in. Sergio Lugo was a five foot nine inch shooting guard. He could've played varsity as a sophomore too, but Butler elected to have him get more game experience by playing on the JV team instead. Sergio and I were the starting guards on the JVs when I was a junior and we played together well. He was a terrific streak shooter and I was pretty good at finding the open man. I did my best to get the ball to Sergio whenever he was open and so did the rest of our teammates. We must have done a pretty good job because as a sophomore Sergio led our JV team in scoring.

The 1974-75 squad didn't have Butler's normal balance. Out of 11 guys on the roster, the other eight were seniors: Chuck Beaver (son of the general who ran George Air Force Base), Mike Halladay, Johnny Castillo, Bill Roes, Steve Williams, Leonard Butts (an energetic five foot seven inch, high jumping, faster than electricity transfer to George Air Force Base from England his senior year), Oscar Lugo (Sergio's cousin) and me. This unbalanced group of one sophomore, two juniors and eight seniors did something no other Butler team had done before, we set a school record for the most wins in a season.

We started the season off with scrimmage victories against Moreno Valley and Norco. (The Moreno Valley scrimmage was great because my first girl friend ever, from way back in the seventh grade, who was now at Moreno Valley after five years in Madrid, Spain, came up with the team as a stat girl and we got reacquainted—though curiously enough my then current girlfriend didn't think much of the idea.) Then came our first pre-league game against Elsinore, the CIF 1A runner-up champion the year before. Elsinore sported two returning All-CIF forwards. No problem. We held their biggest star, six foot six inch forward, John Greer, to four points and dispatched Elsinore in our home opener 70-61.

Balanced scoring, unselfish team play and tremendous defense would be our trademark all season long. (Not surprising, these were the trademarks of all Butler's teams.) Against Elsinore we got 25 points from knuckleball shooting Oscar Lugo, 16 from his cousin Sergio, 15 from Boyd and 9 points from sophomore Tony Anderson in his first high school game. That left 5 points for the seven remaining seniors to contribute collectively. Every game it was the same, three or four guys scoring big while the rest of the team did the other things necessary to win.

There was a running joke our senior year about a comment sportswriter Ernie Castillo would often use: the term was "chipped in." Ernie was our teammate John Castillo's older brother by four years. He was a track man who graduated from VVHS in 1971. Ernie cut his journalistic teeth on the *Jackrabbit Journal* in high school and while taking classes at the community college had been hired as a stringer to write high school sports articles for the *Daily Press.* By the time we were seniors Castillo was working for the newspaper full-time and was closing in on becoming the sports editor. He'd moved up quickly because he also took his own photographs. (Who wouldn't want an employee that could do the work of two people?) He was a natural writer—very clever with figurative language—and he loved to poke subtle jibes at his brother's friends, hence the "chipped in" comments. As in the case of the Elsinore game, where four of eleven guys had done the majority of the scoring and only five points remained for the other seven guys to contribute. Castillo couldn't resist tagging on this last line to his article, "Williams and Halladay scored one basket each, while Kniss chipped in one free throw."

In the second game of the season, we gave Butler his 200th win at VVHS with a crushing 80-36 defeat of Banning. Everyone scored in that game and we all played equal minutes. Team morale was high and we needed it to be high as we were entering our first tournament of the year, the George Ingall's Tournament at Norco High School in Riverside. Since we had beaten Norco handily in the earlier scrimmage, we were confident we would take their tournament title, and sure enough, we did; unfortunately it was only the consolation title.

Against tournament host Norco we were overconfident. We'd beaten them by 30 points just two weeks before and thought we would do so again. Afraid not! Norco out-hustled, out- shot and generally out-played us in a 59-53 showcase game loss the opening night of the tournament. Butler clearly analyzed the situation afterward, which we read in the paper the next morning: "We beat them in a scrimmage…I assume our guys took them for granted." Yep! As usual, Coach was right on top of the situation. That's exactly what happened.

This was also the game I talked back to Coach at half-time when he got on me about a wild pass I'd made that resulted in a turnover and a score for Norco. Talking back was a big mistake, it resulted in me being benched for the remainder of the game (which I liked to fantasize was the reason we lost); and furthermore, I fell into Butler's dog-house for the next couple of games. But get this. In 2001, while interviewing Butler for this book, he reminds me of my big mouth and this little episode that took place back in December of 1974. I figured he'd forgotten it long ago. He must have had hundreds of similar encounters with players since then. Nope! Coach doesn't forget!

The good thing about losing to Norco was it woke us up to reality, we realized we were beatable. It also motivated us to work harder, which we did. We won our next three games in the tournament and took home a nice consolation trophy, and along with it, a more valuable lesson in the dangers of overconfidence. We were 5-1.

In our following outing we ran our record to 6-1 by edging Colton 54-53 at their gym. That was payback for the 69-0 shellacking their football team gave ours earlier in the year. I'll never forget that football game. They were winning 49-0 at half-time and their coach let their players sit in the stands and watch the half-time show rather than take them into the locker room for the usual strategy talk. Butler never would have done anything as unsportsmanlike as that. In our locker room that night, our coach, Wade Sawaia, was screaming, "Their whole team is sitting in the stands right now laughing at us!" I guess they had every right to. Don Markham was their coach then and rumor had it that the way he picked his football team was in the weight room. Tryouts were on the bench press. I heard that he picked the 33 strongest guys then assigned them positions. Whatever it was he did worked because those guys were huge. I played free-safety and I couldn't see over their linemen to see who the quarterback had given the ball to in the backfield. All I could do was run into the group of guys coming at me and try to take down as many as I could at their knees. I think Anthony Munoz, who went on to play at USC and in the NFL for the Cincinnati Bengals, was one of those behemoth linemen I tried to cross body block. I still ache when I think of it.

We played Rim of the World a few days later. It's called Rim of the World High School because it sits on a precipice atop the San Bernardino Mountains between Crestline and Lake Arrowhead, about 7000 feet above sea level, overlooking the vast Inland Empire below. A stone's throw across the highway, the mountains drop straight down thousands of feet and on a clear day it is rumored you can see the Pacific Ocean. It is a picturesque place. Any high school student would love to attend there for the scenery alone.

The story I'm about to tell you is unknown to most of the players on the varsity basketball team that year. We kept it secret for many years. Mr. Butler never knew about it either until he proofread the first draft of this book. He was surprised, but being a man-of-the- world, he was not shocked. And don't think I'm telling you this merely for some gratuitous effect; on the contrary, I'm raising the curtain on this scene because it reflects the mood of the times and gives you a better understanding of the social issues a coach like Butler had to consider as he brought his players into manhood.

If you were coming of age in the early Seventies you might remember how it was (that is if you didn't smoke too much pot and ruin your memory). By April of 1973, President Nixon had ordered American soldiers out of Vietnam. In ending a ten year national fiasco, he hoped to save his administration. He didn't succeed. Richard Nixon, it turns out, was a crook—no matter what he said to the contrary. Just before our senior basketball season began, he was run out of office for his part in the Watergate scandal, though he would escape jail, unlike his henchmen.

The atmosphere in the country was one of distrust and betrayal. Students were disgusted. College campuses were rife with protest movements and civil disobedience was the prevailing philosophy of the day among young people. It hadn't been that long since Nixon's administration provoked the tragedy that resulted in four college students being gunned down by National Guardsmen at Kent State in Ohio. College kids were predominantly antiestablishment.

The spirit of challenging authority naturally trickled down to the high schools across the nation. As teenagers, we were the ones hearing stories from our big brothers—the young soldiers being used as pawns by our government in the killing fields of Southeast Asia. They told us of horrors beyond our comprehension and how many of them had turned to drugs as a way to deaden the pain and ease their consciences. Drugs were flowing into California in the early Seventies through a military black market and soon the mood-altering effects of marijuana, Tai-stick, hashish, and opium were filtering onto high school campuses across the West.

On top of that, the popular effects of mood altering substances had been glorified by the counterculture rock-n-roll music of the Sixties and early Seventies, the music that permeated our homes via the radio every day as we were growing up. We were enveloped by it. TV added to the pop culture glorification of challenging authority also. Add in the natural curiosity of youth and it was pretty much a given that fifty per cent or higher of high school age kids were going to experiment with some sort of drug. The adults had their legal drugs in tobacco and alcohol, why couldn't we have ours? Mr. Butler had taught us about Prohibition and we knew alcohol was once illegal. Marijuana used to be legal, as did cocaine and opium, too. Why weren't they now? Youth have no patience for inconsistency and hypocrisy.

Although we did not know the word, a spirit of Weltschmerz permeated the country then, further complicating our passage through adolescence. As young teens we'd seen the body count in Vietnam rise nightly on the TV news from as far back as we could remember and no amount of euphemism could change someone's dead soldier brother to a mere "casualty." And those of us boys in high school, facing Selective Service when we turned 18, and possibly another draft into the United States Army's killing machine to fight more war in another part of the world against an enemy we didn't know or understand, were doing everything we could to live it up before we graduated and got drafted to go off and die. High school, in essence, had become a place for partying all you could before facing up to your impending adult responsibilities, which to us guys looked pretty close to certain death.

With all that in perspective you might be better able to understand why three guys on Butler's varsity basketball team and another senior in our class ditched school the morning of our game against Rim of the World. We didn't care about school, we wanted adventure and nothing really seemed to matter except having a good time; so, Johnny Castillo, Oscar Lugo, myself and our driver (who will remain unnamed since he wasn't on the basketball team), took off on a road trip the back way through Hesperia, Silverwood Lake, and Lake Gregory to Rim of the World, just to see what it was like up there. On the way up, we smoked about ten joints, one right after another as was our obliterative habit.

When we got to the school we made our way onto the campus and were fortunate enough to get there during a passing period. We stopped a rather friendly group of four girls who right away discerned we were not from their school. (Do desert kids really look that obviously different?) We admitted to being mischievous interlopers and mysteriously teased them along, promising only to reveal out true identities if they would come back for the basketball game that night and meet us. They said they would. We weren't at the school for more than fifteen minutes. We got back in the car, resumed our pot smoking and drove to the nearest fast food restaurant in Lake Gregory to stave off the munchies before heading back to Victorville. When we got back into town a little after noon, we had an hour and a half before the bus would leave for the game.

When we returned to Rim later that afternoon we were zombies. Our unnamed party-car driver was the only smart one of our group; he stayed home and slept off the effects of the all morning marijuana buzz. The girls we hoped to meet never materialized, which was just as well since we ended up embarrassing ourselves anyway.

We weren't any good as you can well imagine after a day of dissipation. Oscar Lugo, our leading scorer, shot back to back air-balls the first two times down the court. He never found his touch and early in the second quarter he was smart enough to feign illness and tell Coach he needed to sit out the rest of the night.

Johnny Castillo looked like a Rodeo clown when Butler put him in. On a breakaway lay-up he dribbled the ball off his foot out of bounds, tripped himself and fell into the drinking fountain cracking open his lip (this was in

Rim's old gym where the walls were three feet away from the court boundary-lines).

I was no better, picking up two quick fouls and missing two easy lay-ups before Butler mercifully returned me to the bench. I had a repeat performance the next time he sent me in and soon after I was on the bench next to Johnny and Oscar for the rest of the game. Fortunately the rest of our team wasn't a bunch of stoners. We won 56-32, and aside from the three dissipaters we looked pretty good doing it.

We three desperadoes slunk off the court afterward. We kept our mouths shut about our little pre-game adventure. Our teammates wouldn't have appreciated our mental preparation. And though we got away with it, amazingly, we learned a lesson all on our own. Never again would we go on a bender like that before a game. Basketball meant too much to us. We laughed quietly between ourselves as we made fun of each other's play, realizing we weren't worth a damn in our dazed and confused state. The rest of the season we saved our partying for after the games.

While Butler was unaware that we were smoking pot during the season he was not oblivious to the fact that drugs were becoming a national problem for the youth of America. It had been that way for some time, though we, just coming into our own, actually thought it was something new. Butler preached about the ill-effects of dissipation to all of his teams. I certainly remember his lectures to us. Even better than that, unlike other beer-swilling, God- cursing, skirt-chasing, chain-smoking coaches, he practiced what he preached. He kept physically fit. Ate right. Didn't imbibe. Coca-Cola was the hard stuff to Butler. A healthy body and sharp mind were always too important to him.

Butler's example eventually did its work on his players though. Generally speaking, by their mid-twenties most of them had outgrown their bad habits and become the men Butler always taught them to be, although with a few it took longer.

But back to the rest of the season.

After Christmas came the annual San Bernardino Kiwanis Classic. At 7-1, we were picked to make it to the finals. If we hadn't lost 57-63 in a tough second round game to eventual tournament champs San Gorgonio, with their future NBA player Steve Johnson, we just might have made those finals. Mediocrely, we came out of the tournament with an even split, losing also to Pacific, but beating Redlands and San Bernardino. We'd achieved Butler's perennial tournament goal—to win as many games as you lost—but it wasn't very satisfying, even if our teammate Clifford Boyd was selected to the All-Tournament team.

When we returned to school after the holidays it was time to start league play and we did it with style by winning ten games in a row. I won't bore you with all the details—I don't want you nodding off. Instead, I'll restrict myself to telling you about two of those ten games.

Our second league game was against Kennedy. I have to tell you about that one because it was the only time all season I got hot. In the second quarter I hit five perimeter jumpers in a row. Not known for my scoring, I had to laugh when I heard the Kennedy players argue about double-teaming me. Little did they know my streak shooting was a fluke. Even better, when we played them in the second round at their gym, they assigned their best defender to guard me. What a riot! I haven't made five shots in a row since.

And then there was our fifth league game against Barstow which could have ended in tragedy but fortunately only ended in mayhem.

In retrospect, the mayhem may have been precipitated by Butler's clairvoyant remarks to sportswriter Ernie Castillo. Butler told Castillo, "Basketball is a small scale war played within certain rules with guys who are paid to make sure the players don't break them." Butler often made those sorts of comments, the metaphoric kind that made us feel we weren't just playing a game, we were battling in a war. We were his platoon. He'd indoctrinated us with the basics. He called them "fundamentals." We followed his orders unequivocally. He trained us so well that our technique was second nature. We didn't have to think, we only had to execute. We glided through games because our training in practice had been so extensive. On the point of leadership, Butler was supreme commander-in-chief with the full trust and loyalty of his troops. Each game was indeed another battle we needed to win in our march toward the league title and the playoffs. Discipline, timing, precision and attention to the slightest detail were all part of Butler's coaching arsenal, but the downside to Butler's high standard of achievement was it made us targets for every other team to shoot at. Good thing they didn't have guns!

Against Barstow, Oscar Lugo had a phenomenal game. Everything he threw up went in. He scored 26 points—all on knuckleballs from long range—and he did it playing only about half the game (since we were blowing Barstow out, the reserves got a lot of minutes). Now there's only one thing Barstow hates more than losing to Victor Valley at home, that's enduring the cocksureness of VVHS shooters. Sometime in the third quarter Oscar got into a taunting match with heckling Barstow students in the crowd. They booed him whenever he scored and he responded by pointing at them then at the scoreboard. After repeating this scene a few times, Coach took him out for the rest of the game, but it was too late, the damage had already been done.

Following the 79-51 debacle, we showered and headed for the bus, the first six of us leaving the locker room together. At Barstow, our driver never parked the bus next to the gym, he always parked below the football stadium at the base of two long flights of stairs. As the six of us reached the top of those dark stairs we could make out the silhouettes of about thirty guys lining both sides of the stairwell leading to the bus.

Hmmm, I guess if we had been smarter, we would have turned around and walked back to the locker room and told Coach what was waiting for us, then waited for security to come and escort us to the bus. Unfortunately, we weren't that smart. Instead, just like Oscar, we were cocky. The six of us thought we could handle the thirty of them, after all, we'd seen all Bruce Lee's movies. We entered the dragon and began to descend the stairs, unable, in our youthful naiveté, to conceive what was about to happen.

Halfway down the stairs, about 90 feet from the top, was a flat landing for grandmas to stop and take a rest from the arduous task of climbing. Bill Roes, our six foot four inch, 210 pound center, was brazenly leading us through the gauntlet of Barstow boys lining the staircase—mostly football and baseball players we found out later. When Roes reached the landing he paused and waited for the rest of us to land too. That's when all hell broke loose.

Out of the side of my vision came a baseball bat. WACK! It hit Roes square across his upper back just below the shoulders and in a split second a full-scale melee was on with fists and feet flying everywhere. The gauntlet converged and we were surrounded, each of us now fighting a minimum of four or five guys.

I saw Oscar tackled to the ground but there was nothing I could do to help. While he was being boot-stomped by as many field goal kickers as Barstow had on their football team, Johnny Castillo, Mike Halladay, Steve Williams, Bill Roes and myself were fighting off our own 20-25 attackers. Halladay and Williams, had trained themselves in a hybrid version of Shoto Kan and Kung Fu. Along the way they had given all of us quasi lessons in martial arts and what I remembered returned in a flash. I kicked out low and hard to bend Barstow knees backwards and used the two fingered peace sign to go for the eyes. I was doing okay until the right heel on my platform shoes broke off, reducing me to uneven clomping as I clumsily kicked out at guys while attempting to edge nearer to the bottom of the steps. Finally, the bus driver saw what was going on above him and hollered. The melee dissolved and the Barstow Improvement Association dispersed in all directions leaving us cut and bleeding and with a lot of ruined clothes hanging off of us. Things might have turned out worse had Roes not taken away the baseball bat from whomever hit him with it and did his best Hank Aaron breaking Babe Ruth's home-run record imitation.

Butler and the rest of the team arrived on the scene about this time. Security was called but the harm was already done. Oscar Lugo was unconscious on the landing and would remain so until an ambulance arrived to haul him away. He ended up having a concussion but no permanent injury (though he did have to sit out three games for precaution's sake—which gave me my only three starts of the year). The police came to our school the next day and took a report. There was a big write up in the paper (which I still have a copy of). The incident was investigated but nothing came of it. Big surprise!

And since this isn't a book about my senior year, I won't go into what we did to get our revenge. It was even uglier than what they did to us and earned me one of the worst rebukes of my life. When Mr. Butler found out what we did he told me, "David, I used to want my son to grow up to be just like you. Not anymore." Another administrator told me the same thing. I wondered if he and Coach Butler had discussed the matter together beforehand. Their lost faith in me was a lot worse punishment than the five days suspension we got.

With Oscar out for three games, other guys had to pick up his offensive slack. He was averaging around 18 points per game. I certainly wasn't going to get that many filling in for him as I was never good for more than 10 points a game on a great night. So Sergio Lugo put up a few extra points, as did Boyd, Williams, and Anderson, and we continued to win without our captain and leading scorer in the lineup. When Oscar returned, just in time for us to play Kennedy the second time, he lit it up like he had never been out, leading us to a 74-48 win.

As I said earlier, we won our first ten league games without a loss, but only barely; our tenth game was a miraculous come from behind win against Antelope Valley at home, where we were down by 18 with only four minutes to go but managed to win by two in regulation. That must have taken too much out of us though, our extreme high after that win was followed by the nadir of our season, a 60-58 loss to Burros in the "snake pit." With the score tied at 58-58, we had the ball with 20 seconds to go. All we had to do was run down the clock and take the last shot. If we missed it, at least we'd get a three minute overtime. If only it had turned out that way.

Driving to the basket, I was cut off by one of the Blanche brothers so I pulled up for a jumper, remembering only after I had left my feet that Butler didn't want us to shoot too early; an early missed shot would give Burros enough time to go down and score. Hanging in the air, with no place to go but down to an ups-and downs call, I passed instead to a teammate, but my ill-timed pass was unexpected causing it to be bobbled then stolen by Burros guard Billy Doremus, who took it back up court and hit a 12 foot jumper like he was Jerry West against the Celtics to put them ahead 60-58 with six seconds to go. Sergio Lugo's desperation shot at the buzzer failed to retie the game, sending us home with our first league loss.

I felt like crap after the game and blamed myself for the loss. I felt like I could cry, but knew I had to be a man about the whole first league loss thing. Besides, Butler always preached that no single mistake ever decided a game, it just seemed like it did when the mistake happened at the end. In Butler's view, all the mistakes added up in a loss, and a first quarter miscue that led to an opponent's score was just as critical as one that happened in the last two seconds. So at least I had that to comfort me, though it wasn't really working.

Butler gave us the after game speech to put things in perspective. We missed eight free-throws. We turned the ball over too many times. Our big men sat out a number of minutes in the second half due to foul trouble. All these factors added up to our loss. He didn't mention my bad pass at all. A little later, as we dressed after showering, Butler walked the quiet rows and did his best to console us. When he got to me, sitting alone in a row by myself, he calmly said, "Now you know why I always say not to get up in the air with nowhere to go," and patted me on the shoulder and walked away. No finger-pointing. No blame. No harsh words. Just a statement of fact that I clearly understood as a lesson to learn.

When I went on to coach high school basketball I taught my players the same thing—don't get caught up in the air with no where to go. I also tried to handle frustrating losses with the same class as Ollie Butler.

The next morning in the sports page, we were not surprised to read the following Butler comments: "I'm still convinced we're the best team. We won ten straight before the loss and I feel we can win three straight after it."

We did, ending league play at 13-1 with an overall record of 22-4.

In the first round of the CIF playoffs we were bracketed against the Ramona Rams of Riverside, a team we matched up with evenly in the scouting report. I always had a good feeling about playing Ramona. They were my first high school opposition when I played on the sophomore football team. I got my first interception against them which kept them from scoring again and led to our come from behind victory when we marched eighty yards down the field in the last four minutes to tie the score 6-6, before golden-toe Petersen kicked the extra point to give us a 7-6 win in the last twenty seconds. I also scored my first varsity touchdown against Ramona as a junior when we opened the season against them in a 27-14 win at home. *Bring on the Ramona Rams, we can't lose.*

Boy did my intuition turn out to be cattywampus. On Tuesday night, February 24, 1975, my high school basketball career came to an end. As it turned out, we didn't match up well against Ramona at all. They raced out to a 33-13 first quarter lead behind Speedy Brown and never looked back. Oscar Lugo was the only one of us who could find the basket with any consistency, he finished with 21 points. The rest of the team suffered through our worst game of the entire season. Great timing! We lost by 20 points. No way to end a record-breaking season (we were the first VVHS team ever to win 22 games in a season).

To lighten our spirits in the locker room after the game, Butler took the blame on himself. He told us, "Nobody can take away what you did this year. We had a good season. I had a bad last game. I'm going home now and figure out a group of players for next year."

I sat there wondering how he figured it was his fault. He hadn't missed a shot or thrown a ball away or committed a stupid foul or let his man beat him to the basket. Yet that was Butler for you, the consummate competitor: undaunted, unvanquished, just temporarily set back; and now Butler was going to go home and start figuring out how to surround Sergio Lugo, Clifford Boyd and Tony Anderson with the right guys to make a run at the title next year. Amazing.

Years later, going through my own coaching initiation, I came to understand how Butler was able to shift the blame for losses onto his own shoulders. He told me, "When you guys went on the court, you were me. If you made a bad pass, I made a bad pass. If you fouled, I fouled. I wanted you to play as close to perfect as possible because that's the way I always tried to play when I stepped on the floor. That's why if you played badly it was my fault, I hadn't prepared you well enough. You were me on that court."

Well, even though we lost our first round CIF game we had given Butler a school record and a second consecutive Golden League Championship. In his mid-forties now, Butler was seasoned, tested, and tempered. He was as knowledgeable as any high school coach in the game and in the next eight years he would lead the Jackrabbits to eight more successive league crowns. There was no doubt in any one's mind that Butler's Victor Valley Jackrabbits were a lean, mean, green and white basketball machine.

VVHS 1976-78

Clifford Boyd made All-CIF at forward his junior year. He and the Lugo cousins also made All-Golden League. Now seniors, Clifford and Sergio had a lot to prove. As juniors both were being recruited by a number of colleges. Tony Anderson, who had played spectacularly as a sophomore, was returning too, and the local paper had dubbed these guys the "Big Three." Along with the Big Three were: Don White, Larry Fealy, Barry Stonesifer, Tim Serrano, Mike Sawaia, Mark Halbe, David Manson, and William Lightner. Our school record of 22 wins in a season wouldn't survive more than a year with these guys around. Again, VVHS was the odds on favorite to take the league crown.

The 1975-76 season started with Victor Valley pounding it's first two opponents, Norco and Damien, by a combined score of 164 points to 96. Lugo, Boyd and Anderson were dominant and the bench play was magnificent. Butler would use ten players regularly this whole season, and in the latter half of the 1970s would become a big proponent of going deep into his bench to win.

When VVHS clobbered defending CIF 1A Champion, Banning High School, 76-44 (and if I may add, since you probably forgot, we beat Banning by 44 points the year before to give them their only loss on their way to that CIF 1A Championship) in their third game of the season, it gave them the confidence to believe that they could also make it all the way to the finals. But after a fourth victory over Riverside North, a piece of humble pie was served up.

Elsinore, with its six foot six inch, two time All-CIF center, John Greer—who we had held to four points the previous year in our season opener—proved why he was an All-CIF selection. In the first round of the Banning "Block B" Tournament, Greer dominated the inside in leading Elsinore to a 75-73 overtime win. The game could have gone either way. Lugo, Boyd and Anderson all played well enough but collectively as a team they didn't get the job done. No excuses. They were now 4-1 and the burden of going undefeated was removed.

Victor Valley won it's next two games in the Banning tournament against Bloomington and Banning—defeating Banning for the second time in the season, this time 112-37 to take the Consolation Championship. In doing so, Tony Anderson set a new school single game rebounding record, the first of many he would set before graduating. He pulled down 28 boards, besting Greg Hyder's 1965 record of 26. The Rabbits also set a new single game scoring record with their 112 points.

The Kiwanis tournament was better to VVHS this year than in recent ones. The Rabbits exceeded Butler's goal of an even split by going 3-1. Their only loss was to defending tournament champ, San Gorgonio 68-74. The three games they won were against Ronnie Lott's Eisenhower Eagles 65-49, the Hemet Bulldogs 56-50, and the Fontana Steelers 61-56. This put VVHS at 8-2 for the month of December. Not a bad start considering every game was played on the road.

Victor Valley's first home game of the season against Moreno Valley was also their last pre-league game. It was a barn-burner as they say. VVHS just held on to win 65-59. At 9-2, the Jackrabbits were ready for league.

Their first Golden League contest was against Kennedy. Using the press and the fast break VVHS ran by the Spartans 78-45. Anderson, Boyd and Lugo led a balanced scoring attack with 19, 18 and 16 points respectively. Point guard Barry Stonesifer was now contributing consistently on offense too, he had 10. These four guys did virtually all the scoring for the rest of the year.

Next, VVHS shot down the Antelope Valley Antelopes 67-58 like hunters on opening day; then, for the first time in three years, the Rabbits bombed the Burros 76-64 in Ridgecrest. In a sweet moment of nostalgia the following week, the Rabbits gave Butler his 300th career coaching win with a tough victory over long time league rival Barstow 54-48. The winning continued against Quartz Hill 55-54, Apple Valley 69-43, and Kennedy again 64-60.

The Rabbits were 8-0 in league when Clifford Boyd, a three year varsity starter, set a new school record in scoring, going over 1000 points. He was also closing in on 1000 rebounds—although he would ultimately fall a little bit short. The Rabbits hadn't lost since the Kiwanis Tournament. Everything was going their way; but Butler, who says he isn't superstitious, began worrying about a letdown. He didn't have to wait long.

Antelope Valley, ever a thorn in Butler's side under alcoholic coach Al Blankenship (it was no secret to anyone), handed VVHS their first league loss 63-60. Butler, in a rankled moment, pointed his finger at the bench. His reserves saw more playing time than any other bench in the league but lately they had been producing more negatives than positives. Butler felt too many games had been closer than they should have been. "The bench hasn't been doing the job," Butler lamented after the loss. "The guts of modern basketball is the bench."

Apparently that was what the bench needed to read in the papers. The rest of the year they played superbly. VVHS cruised to five more league wins and won the crown with a 13-1 league record, the same record we had won it with in '75. At 22-3 they were highly seeded going into the CIF playoffs.

In their first round game, Tony Anderson dazzled the college scouts in attendance with a 28 point performance in a win over Los Altos. Ironically, the scouts were there to watch Boyd and Lugo, not Anderson. Anderson, who was plagued with knee problems at the beginning of the year and sat out a few games early on, was only beginning to emerge as a bona fide college prospect his junior year, he wasn't nearly as well known among recruiters as were seniors Boyd and Lugo though he had averaged a respectable 18 points per game all year. Still, he was in the background behind Boyd, who had ascended to become Victor Valley's all time leading rebounder and scorer. Against Los Altos Anderson emerged from Boyd's shadow. The scouts were pleased with what they saw.

In the second round of the playoffs VVHS was matched against the Ramona Rams, the team that knocked them out in the first round of the playoffs the previous year. Based on their 23-3 record, Victor Valley was confident against Ramona. The Rabbits had become an excellent team in every sense of the word. While they relied heavily on their three big guns, the rest of the players provided the necessary intangibles that make the difference between a good and a great team. A lot of people thought Victor Valley had the complete package required to make it to the finals. There was a lot of talk...unfortunately, that's all it turned out to be.

The Ramona Rams had Victor Valley's number for the second year in a row. Sergio Lugo, an 87 percent free throw shooter for his career, missed his first five free throws and the rest of the squad didn't do much better. Although the Rabbits scored more field goals than the Rams, they were outscored at the charity stripe in a 57-54 loss. Butler hated it when his teams missed free throws, always emphasizing the word "free." He was the best free throw shooting teacher in high school basketball, once demonstrating how "free" they were by making ten in a row blindfolded, and also making 188 in a row in a competition with Oscar Lugo who had hit a consecutive 169. While Butler was disappointed that such a talented team had to exit the playoffs so early, he was practical about the loss, "You don't deserve to win if you can't make your free throws." They finished the year 23-4, setting a new school single season win record.

Sergio Lugo and Clifford Boyd made both the All-Golden League and the All-CIF teams. Boyd, a top student as well as an athlete, would go on to a four year career at the academically challenging University of Redlands. Lugo, went to the community college, then transferred to Southern Utah, where he missed the last cut because he was only five foot ten and they wanted a six foot four inch guard they could post up.

On a side note, Sergio's cousin Oscar told me that after Sergio got cut he started playing intramural ball. After lighting up the intramural league for around 40 points a night for a couple of weeks, word got back to the Southern Utah coaches that there was a tremendous shooter playing intramurals that they might be able to use on their team. They came to look. "Hey, isn't that the guy we cut?" They didn't change their minds though. Apparently a five foot ten inch Mexican-American guard who could give them 20-40 points a game didn't fit their prototype. No wonder Southern Utah hasn't ever done much. Maybe they need to change their philosophy.

Over the past two seasons, Butler's teams had gone 45-9. He was doing everything right, plus he was blessed with a throng of talented players. Most of his bench players would have started for other teams in the league. He had just led the Rabbits to their third consecutive league title and was only coming into his prime at the midway point in a 28 season coaching career at VVHS. His 15th season would be his best yet.

In Tony Anderson's sensational senior year he all but erased Victor Valley fans' memories of the talented tandem of Boyd and Lugo. Not only did Anderson end up the CIF 2A Player of the Year, he was the MVP of all three tournaments the Rabbits played in and broke all of Clifford Boyd's newly set records in scoring 1,218 points and grabbing 1047 rebounds in three years on the varsity. By the time he was through in high school he had averaged 26 points per game and ended up moving into fifth place in the CIF record books for his career rebounding stats. Coach Butler says he was recruited by at least 100 major colleges. Not bad for a six foot four inch forward with limited lateral movement. What's more amazing is that if you saw Tony today, he's in such great shape that he could probably put up similar numbers.

With Anderson in 1976-77 were: Stonesifer, Sturdivant, Sawaia, Lightner, and Manson. Duane Gatson, Craig Yankaskas, Chris Alvarado, Bob Collins, and Leo Carpenter. And this year, for a pleasant change, Butler had a true center in six foot eight inch John Newman. Instead of starting three guards as he had the previous season, he started two: Stonesifer and Sturdivant, who Butler called, "the finest pair of passers I ever had at Victor Valley."

These two veteran seniors were athletes who both possessed something Butler never believed he could teach: innate court awareness. They each had uncanny peripheral vision, tremendous poise and unselfish attitudes. Without Stonesifer and Sturdivant, Butler doesn't think Tony Anderson would have been the CIF 2A Player of the Year so instrumental were they in getting Anderson the ball when he was open.

With Anderson at forward, Newman at center, and Stonesifer and Sturdivant at guards, Butler moved junior, William Lightner, into the starting line-up at the other forward. Butler calls Lightner, "one of the toughest small forwards I ever had at Victor Valley." Butler stayed with this line-up most of the season.

And then there was the bench, by now the Jackrabbits' real programmatic strength. Some coaches only like to use six or seven guys the whole game. They don't like the talent drop-off they usually get when the eighth, ninth, or tenth man comes into the game. Not Butler. He developed his bench by teaching the less talented players how to be effective during their spot-playing stretches. He often used ten players to win night in and night out. Because of this philosophy, Butler's Jackrabbits wore teams down. He strategically inserted role players to come in and change the tempo of the game while giving his starters some deserved rest. Come crunch time, these backup players whom Butler used consistently all year, weren't nervous or hesitant. They didn't play a lot, but they played regularly and knew their role, which was to come in and give two to three minutes of base-line to base-line non-stop effort before returning to the bench. Butler's backups lived for those stretches and you can be sure whomever Butler summoned to come off his bench was ready and waiting to give that all-out effort when called upon.

At the same time the Rabbits were opening their season this year, convicted serial killer Gary Gilmore was in the news. He had already been tried, convicted and given the death penalty but his mother kept appealing for a life sentence against the prosecuting attorney who was desperately working to get him executed. Weekly, it seemed, Gilmore's mother would win a temporary stay of execution for her son. However, she was merely postponing the inevitable. She won some battles but wouldn't win the war. During the 1976-77 season, many Jackrabbits opponents wished, too, for a stay of execution; unfortunately their mommies couldn't help them. All season long the Tony Anderson led Rabbits dealt out sentences that were punitive, unmerciful and swift.

Victor Valley won their first three games before losing 51-63 to Moreno Valley in the finals of the San Dimas Tournament. William Lightner made the All-Tournament team and Tony Anderson was its Most Valuable Player. They set things right a week later though when they avenged themselves against Moreno Valley in a rematch. David Manson was the difference in that game, coming off the bench to score 16 points.

Then came the inaugural game of the Victor Valley Kiwanis Classic, an idea Butler borrowed from San Bernardino. The past two summers Butler had coached an Olympic Development team consisting of big name players from the Inland Empire. In his first season he had been named Coach of the

Year, while Steve Johnson, playing for Butler, was selected the Player of the Year. Johnson went on to star in the PAC 8 at Oregon State and then to the NBA for a good many seasons. It was during Butler's second Olympic Development summer league that he concocted his plan to host a Christmas tournament at Victor Valley that would showcase local and regional talent.

The Victor Valley Kiwanis Classic had its debut on December 20, 1976. Only eight teams were invited the first year but Butler had plans to develop this into a more prestigious event in the years to come. Victor Valley got off to a good tournament start with a 99-59 romp over Coachella Valley. Their other two victories were equally impressive, propelling the Rabbits to win their own tournament and at the same time deliver Butler his 250th win at VVHS. Barry Stonesifer was named Most Valuable Defensive Player, while Tony Anderson, for the second time in two tournaments, was the Most Valuable Player overall.

The day after Christmas the San Bernardino Kiwanis Tournament began. As they were the previous year, Victor Valley was the top seed and they finally lived up to their ranking. There would be no close losses this time around. In the finals, VVHS defeated Ronnie Lott's Eisenhower Eagles again, as they had last year in the third place game. Victor Valley placed four players on the All-Tournament team. Dansby Sturdivant was the Most Inspirational Player. Barry Stonesifer was All Tournament for the second year in a row. William Lighter made it too. And the Most Valuable Player award, for his third consecutive tournament, went to none other than Tony Anderson.

When the holidays ended and the Jackrabbits were ready to start league, they were ranked number one in CIF 2A polls. At 12-1, VVHS had surpassed the 11-1 record set by the 1964-65 Rabbits, to give the team its best start under Butler, another record that would be broken before too long. Records were big with Butler, he'd been compiling statistics since his very first job at St. Joseph's. Ever the consummate statistician, Butler now had in his employ his eldest daughter, Jana. With three daughters ahead of his son, he didn't' want them feeling left out. As soon as they got into high school he trained each daughter to understand the nuances of the game and the statistical nomenclature: the difference between a loose ball recovery and a steal, the difference between a bad pass and a fumble, the difference between a rebound and a tip, etc. Jana had eagle-eyes. She rarely missed an assist and could be counted on to know at all times how many fouls each player had (on both teams). She was her father's right hand, coaches Scoggin and McDonald were his left hand.

Willie McDonald was another former Butler player who'd come back to teach and coach at VVHS. He played for Butler between 1962-65, went to community college for most of the next year then joined the military. In

1968, after a two year stretch in Viet Nam, he returned to Victorville and wasn't sure what he wanted to do with his life. Coach Butler didn't take long to help McDonald figure it out.

Unknown to McDonald, Butler sent his transcripts to coaching pal Bob Kloppenberg at Cal Western University in San Diego, which got McDonald an offer of a full scholarship, sight unseen, to play basketball, all on Butler's verbal recommendation. McDonald was a six foot five inch power forward. He couldn't believe it when Butler told him what he'd done.

According to McDonald, "Ollie Butler couldn't have had a more direct influence on my career." McDonald went to Cal Western, starred on the basketball team and decided to become a history teacher and coach like his mentor Butler, the same script Steve Scoggin followed. And like he did for Scoggin in 1972, Butler paved the way for McDonald to return to VVHS in 1973 by letting Superintendent Harvey Irwin know he had a qualified young teacher and coach available to improve the quality of instruction at Victor Valley. Butler also reminded Irwin how important it was that VVHS hire African-American role models like Willie McDonald.

As Butler and McDonald coached and taught together over the years, their relationship shifted from the player-coach model to one of true friendship. Butler chuckles when he describes their latter years coaching together as being like a marriage: "We used to finish each other's sentences," Butler said.

Butler's other assistant coach, JV head coach Steve Scoggin, was another protégé. I already told you a little about Steve, but I'll add a bit more. Butler says McDonald and Scoggin were, "the two best assistants I ever had in 35 years of coaching." You'll remember Steve's older brother Fella played with McDonald for Butler, too. Like Willie and Fella, who both became teachers and coaches, Steve's career was equally effected by Butler's influence. After four years at Whittier College on a basketball scholarship Steve returned to VVHS a year ahead of McDonald. Under Butler he learned what it took to become a head coach and in 1978 he moved on to become one himself for the next twenty years.

"When I started out," Scoggin said, "I wanted to be just like Ollie Butler and although my career doesn't hold a candle to his, I owe most of my success to what I learned from him. He was a great coach, very much in the John Wooden vein."

But enough reminiscing, which you can probably tell by now I like to do a lot of, let me get back to the 1976-77 season.

Victor Valley dominated league play like never before. They only had two close games, the last two, against Apple Valley 68-59 and Kennedy 50-47; other than that they pounded everyone by 20 points or more. They were a perfect 14-0 in league and by playoff time they were riding an amazing 22 game winning streak and had already set another school record for most wins in a season at 25-1, with four more games still to go in the playoffs.

The Jackrabbits were seeded number one going into CIF, thereby drawing a first round bye. After nearly two weeks off, they met the Indio Rajahs in the second round and Butler worried there might be some rustiness. This time his worries proved groundless as the Jackrabbits showed no need for Rustoleum in blowing past the Rajahs. Anderson scored 41 points while USC's Bob Boyd looked on scouting him. Boyd drooled enviously, "We could use him tomorrow against UCLA. That kid could help us right now!" Anderson, who as I have already mentioned had been recruited by a legion of major colleges his senior year, was currently leaning toward USC or Louisville. Ironically, at the midnight hour, Tony chose UCLA instead, who up to that point had only shown minimal interest. He never regretted the decision.

In the third round (also known as the quarterfinals), VVHS stormed by Alta Loma 63-46, but this would mark the end of easy playoff wins. In the semifinals they would need a huge team effort if they were to slay the giant they faced in West Covina. West Covina's Workman High School had two All-CIFers in seven foot center, David McGuire, and shooting guard, David Morales. Butler's game-plan was to put defensive specialist Dansby Sturdivant on Morales and have Anderson, Lightner and Newman triple team McGuire whenever possible. The strategy proved effective. Both McGuire and Morales were held far below their season averages and Sturdivant came through with his best defensive effort of the year, prompting Butler to remark, "He played Morales like a hungry dog on a juicy bone." When the game ended 50-49 in favor of Victor Valley, the 1000 plus fans who had made the trip to West Covina began chanting "Long Beach Arena, Long Beach Arena." After 15 years, Butler had finally gotten his team to the CIF finals.

At 28-1, number one seed Victor Valley High School was the favorite in the championship game against Channel Islands—the sixth seed entering the playoffs. But being the favored team didn't mean much to Channel Islands, who was hot, having overachieved all the way to the finals behind their star guard, George Emverzo, a Sergio Lugo type shooter and hustler. Just like Victor Valley, this was the first time in school history for Channel Islands to make it to the CIF finals and they didn't expect to lose any more than Victor Valley did after such a long arduous quest. Each team probably hoped the other would be nervous playing in front of so many people in such a big venue. Each team probably hoped the championship was their destiny. Wishing each other luck, as they had done all year long before each game, Butler, Scoggin and McDonald shook hands and walked through the tunnel from the locker room onto the arena floor. Presumably the Channel Islands coaches did the same.

From the beginning to the end it was a war. Both teams took the first quarter to settle down but once they finally did it was an exciting affair. Unfortunately, in the second quarter the Jackrabbits got into foul trouble. The calls tipped in favor of Channel Islands. The scorebook shows Channel Islands went to the free throw line 35 times in comparison to Victor Valley's 17. Butler thought the calls could have been more balanced but admitted that his team was very aggressive. Anderson fouled out in the fourth quarter. Lightner and Newman spent too much time on the bench in foul trouble. Then, when it counted most, Victor Valley missed seven of their 17 free throws which turned out to be the difference in the game. They lost 71-68.

After a loss like that, you'd think there'd be a lot of gnashing of teeth in the loser's locker room but it wasn't like that at all. No one was crying, much. No one was cursing, much. No one was abusing locker room equipment, at all. The players were fairly calm and collected while Butler preached his message of perspective: "You're as good a basketball team as there is," he told the players. "Don't give up just because you lost a ball game. Remember the 28 you won, not the two you lost. Believe that you can learn from this loss, and maybe we can make it back here next year and turn it around."

Later in the after game press conference with sportswriters from big papers like the *Los Angeles Times*, the *Herald Examiner* and the *Orange County Register* gathered around, Butler said he felt like Bobby Knight when he spoke at the team banquet following Indiana's 1975-76 NCAA Championship season. Quoting Knight he said, "Take a long look at these fellows because it will be a long time before you see another bunch like them."

In 1977-78, Victor Valley went through three big changes.

The first was assistant coach Steve Scoggin leaving VVHS to take his first head coaching job at Serrano, a new high school opening in the foothills below Wrightwood, CA. (Willie McDonald became the head JV coach.) In his first year, Scoggin took the Diamondbacks to the Pinion League title and then to the CIF playoffs. They finished with a record of 16-9. Scoggin was so successful at Serrano that the next year he was able to move up in the ranks when he was offered the head coach job at Glendora High School.

The second change involved re-leaguing. Victor Valley was bumped from the Golden League into the San Andreas League with Hemet, Cajon, Yucaipa, La Sierra, Norte Vista, Moreno Valley, and Apple Valley. Butler welcomed the change of pace though he didn't like the break with tradition. Victor Valley had been in the Golden League longer than anyone could remember.

And the third big change was a new rule. It affected Butler more than either of the other two.

The National Basketball Federation, in response to a proliferation of abuse by coaches, instituted a new rule that confined coaches to their seat for most of the game. Locally, some critics called it the "Butler rule." Butler, an enthusiastic and highly motivational coach, was widely known for his sideline antics. Unlike his primary mentor, the stoic John Wooden, Butler had an animated approach to game coaching and the new rule, some felt, was implemented to keep coaches like Butler restricted to a more passive role in the game. This rule, the predecessor of the coach's box, had six stipulations for when a coach could leave his seat during a game: (1) if a time-out was called; (2) if the clock was stopped due to a dead ball; (3) if a player was injured; (4) if the coach was signaling a play; (5) if the coach was responding enthusiastically to a great play; (6) if the coach was going to verify statistics at the score table. If a coach got off the bench for any reason other than these, he would be issued a technical foul.

To understate the matter, Butler thought the new rule "excessive."

Other than those three changes, everything else remained about the same for Victor Valley. They would terrorize the new league the same way they had the old one with their trademark brand of fast-breaking, pass-oriented ball-control offense and high pressure defense. In preseason they were picked to win the league title. They were also picked as a top seed in every tournament they entered. They were again forecast to advance far into the playoffs.

They came through on each prediction.

Although you would think it impossible to replace a High School All-American like Tony Anderson, plus All-Leaguers like Stonesifer and Sturdivant, Butler managed to fill the holes in the program that their graduations created. Coming back from the CIF finalist team were William Lightner (All-League), David Manson, Duane Gatson and Craig Yankaskas. They would be Butler's team leaders this year. Moving up in the program from the sophomore and JV teams were: Harry Bee, Mark Ferguson, Keith Warren, Mike Torpey, Scott Miller, David Anderson, Tyree Brown and Duane's twin brother, Darryl Gatson.

The season began with an unexpected guest speaker, Billie Joe Mason of Bradley University, now with the Harlem Globetrotters. Butler is hazy on how Mason came to speak, but he thinks Nate Ruffin, a counselor then at Victor Valley High and a part-time minister, must have put in a word with Mason to coax him into talking to the team. Between engagements, Mason, who was staying at the Holiday Inn in Victorville, came down to the gym in a tuxedo and delivered an inspirational lecture to the practicing players. Although Butler had given his players the same message many times, coming from a Harlem Globetrotter it seemed fresh and carried special significance.

"To succeed in basketball," Mason told them, "requires five things: (1) you must listen to your coach; (2) you must be intensely determined to succeed; (3) you must practice constantly; (4) you must develop sound fundamental technique; (5) you must be self-disciplined." Then Mason went on to connect basketball with education, something Butler had also been repeating for 20 years. "Basketball is just a game. It's school that develops your mind. To be a success in life, you need to develop your mind."

Butler was glad Mason had come by. Always an educator first and a coach second, Butler knew his players needed to hear that same message from as many successful adults as possible so it would sink in. There was more to success in life than being a good basketball player.

A few days later, on December 9, 1977, an unusually late start date, VVHS opened with a close 48-43 home win against San Gorgonio. Butler termed it "the roughest game in my 20 years of coaching. A couple of times I thought the referees were going to measure for a first down."

VVHS followed with three more wins before faltering in the finals of their own Kiwanis Classic. Juggernaut Chaparral High School of Las Vegas, ranked 16th in the nation, beat VVHS 81-78. To Butler a three point loss to a team of such high caliber was almost a moral victory. Duane Gatson made the All-Tournament team and teammate William Lightner was selected the tournament's Most Valuable Defensive Player.

At the San Bernardino Kiwanis Tournament, VVHS was favored to repeat as champs and probably would have if "atrocious officiating," as Butler termed it, hadn't contributed to a second round 55-53 defeat at the hands of the Eisenhower Eagles.

At this point in his career, Butler had established himself as one of high school basketball's greatest antagonists of bad referees. He despised out of shape officials who couldn't get up and down the court to the right positions to make the critical calls. He was critical of those who didn't know the rules well. He never cared much for refs who couldn't separate their egos from the objective facts of the game. Though a few officials liked Butler because he made their job interesting and challenging, he was the worst nightmare for many others. Some downright feared him. Others could be intimidated by him. There were also a few who loathed him. (You'll meet two of them later.) Butler had memorized the CIF rule book the same way he had memorized the important facts of history. Yet, with all this acrimony between Butler and bad officials, he never liked blaming them for a loss though he made an exception in this case. Despite the sour loss to Eisenhower, the Rabbits went 3-1 in the tournament and took fifth place. Mark Ferguson and William Lightner made the All-Tournament team.

Victor Valley, new to the San Andreas League, wasted no time in duplicating their undefeated league run of the previous season, going 14-0 again. They were unstoppable against every team in the league, averaging a 20 point margin of victory in their 14 league games. Only one game was close, Apple Valley in the last game of the regular season. For most of the game it looked like Apple Valley was going to spoil Victor Valley's perfect league record. They jumped out to a 15 point first half lead and held onto it more or less all the way through the first three quarters; but under the tenacious strategizing of the experienced Butler, who had seen VVHS through many a comeback over the years, the Jackrabbits were able to whittle down Apple Valley's lead late in the fourth quarter and eventually surpass them to win 60-57. This gave Butler 19 wins in 20 games against Apple Valley, their only win coming in 1972, 82-80.

At 21-2, the Rabbits entered the CIF playoffs seeded number three. Butler liked this better than last year when they were seeded number one, there was less pressure on his boys. In the first round they pummeled Workman 78-44. Last year Workman almost kept them from the finals when they played them in West Covina. Playing them at home this year made a big difference in the margin of victory. In the second round VVHS faced elimination. It took a late two-pointer and David Manson's two free throws with three seconds to go to pull out the game against Bellflower 56-53. In the quarterfinals they had an easier time of it, handling San Marino 70-56. And then, for the second year in a row, they found themselves at the Long Beach Arena, where both the semifinals and the finals would be held.

VVHS got their first win at the Long Beach Arena in their semifinal game against Saugus, but it was such an ugly win Butler was almost embarrassed about it. Both teams played the whole night as if they wanted to throw the game away. Luckily for VVHS, Saugus played worse, losing 53-49. Surprisingly, this semi-final victory set up a rematch of last year's final game with Channel Islands, who this year was the favorite as the defending champion. Butler hoped the Rabbits' underdog status would work to their advantage.

I wish I could tell you that Victor Valley redeemed themselves against Channel Islands, but I can't. The truth is Channel Islands blew them out early, and though VVHS did everything it could to fight back and make a game of it, they lost by 11 points, 69-58. The officiating was superb. There were no disproportionate foul calls. The players played their hearts out. Channel Islands was simply the better team. Butler had no complaints, only self-criticism. He suggested the Rabbits might have done better had he employed a different defense, "My sliding 2-1-2 zone was no better than a leaky sieve."

Afterward Butler had high praise for Channel Islands. He had known it would take a supreme team effort to beat them because they had "super ballplayers at every position." They were actually better than the team the Rabbits faced last year in the finals while his team wasn't quite as strong. In the press conference afterward Butler acknowledged that Channel Islands was the best team in the 2A division, and felt that they could probably beat the best team in the 3A division. "Heck, they're probably the third or fourth best team in 4A." Perhaps this was just a ploy to console his players though. Losing isn't quite as bad when you are beaten by the very best. The Rabbits ended their season 25-3.

As the team bus prepared to leave the Long Beach Arena after losing in the finals for the second year in a row, Butler did what all great coaches instinctively know how to do—put the loss into focus: "It's times like these when you have deep dark thoughts about still coaching. Later, you go home, sip some coke, look at the stats and think of the good season. The next day the sun comes up and you're ready to go again. That's the thing that's really great, there's always another season coming up."

Recently, I ran into Craig Yankaskas, the sixth man and sometimes starter on the 1977-78 Jackrabbit squad as well as a back-up guard and spot player on the Tony Anderson led 1976-77 Jackrabbit team. I asked him about playing for Butler, about his back-to-back trips to the finals, and what he liked most about playing for Coach Butler.

"The practices," he said. "I remember like it was yesterday. I'd come out of the locker room after changing into my gym clothes and go straight to where Coach had the practice schedule taped to the wall to see what drills we were going to do. My favorite was continuous fast-break. I miss that twenty minutes in practice more than the games, more than my girlfriend cheering in the stands, more than going to the finals two years in a row. I miss practice more than anything else. Sometimes when I run into Coach at a game, I ask him, 'When are we having our next practice?' Coach always replies, 'Tomorrow at 3:30.'"

"Yank"—as he is affectionately referred to by his friends—captures here the nostalgic feelings most of Butler's former players have for him and his program.

VVHS 1979-89

Between 1975 and 1978 Butler's teams went 98-14, so it was a pretty ho-hum year in 1978-79 when they went 17-6, though for Butler this was as memorable a year as any of his 20+ win seasons, but not for any reasons you might guess. The milestone that made this year memorable for Butler was that his son Mike began school. Now Ollie could officially begin counting the years until Mike would hit high school and try out for the team. When Mike was a toddler it had become a ritual for Sharon to hand him to Ollie after a win so Butler could hoist Mike up onto his shoulders and carry him around as he congratulated and was congratulated by colleagues, players, fans, parents, and friends. Mike was getting a little too big for that now. He had the run of the gym at six years old. Instead of letting his dad carry him on his shoulders, he preferred to celebrate a win by grabbing a basketball and shooting, even if he could only hit the bottom of the net.

"I was about six years old when I first thought about playing basketball for Dad," Mike said. "I was a hellion running around the gym. Mom couldn't catch me. I loved watching Dad get crazy on the sidelines. I knew I wanted that crowd yelling for me."

Ollie Butler could tell his son had the makings of a basketball player.

In 1978-79, the Jackrabbit roster had four returning lettermen from the team that went to the finals. They were: Mike Torpey, Scott Miller, Harry Bee and David Anderson. Joining these veterans were incoming sophomores: Taylor Conlon, Billy Robinson and Jeff Oldfield. Butler added six others who'd moved up through the program: Danny Kurtz, Paul McCloney, Andy Jefferson (later the number one black motocross rider in the world), Carlos Jones, Pat Fealy and Guy Hunter.

As an incoming sophomore, Billy Robinson got off to a bad start with Butler in the summer. "Coach Butler kicked me out of the gym the first day of summer ball. I came in with my hat on backward, cussing and acting tough. I really thought I was something. Butler threw me the hell out. That was just what I needed. We never had a problem after that."

As they had done for the past five years, Victor Valley won four of their first five games, their single loss coming in their own Kiwanis Classis in the semifinals against Rancho of Las Vegas. The Rabbits settled for third place. Harry Bee was the sole Victor Valley player to make All-Tournament, and he did so with distinction, winning the "Mr. Hustle" trophy. (This was the last year Victor Valley hosted their own Kiwanis tournament. Too many prestigious tournaments were drawing the big name schools. Not enough quality teams were signing up for the VVHS Kiwanis Classis so Butler decided to drop it.)

Then came the embitterment!

Just after Christmas the Rabbits entered the San Bernardino Kiwanis Tournament as the number two seed, and in the first round were paired against the number three seed. Butler was incensed and vociferous in his opposition to the bracketings. This was not the way to run a tournament. He could not understand placing the number one, two, three, and four teams against each other in the first round the way tournament officials had. He suspected they were trying to help the local teams finish higher in the prestigious tournament's final rankings. Back then the tournament was double-elimination which meant as soon as you lost two you were ousted (today it's a round-robin format). As mentioned earlier, Butler's goal for tournaments was to play the maximum number of games possible and win at least as many games as you lost. This year, for the first time ever, the Jackrabbits were eliminated in two games, first losing to Redlands 74-76, and then to Las Vegas 76-60. Irate that his perennial tournament-title-contending team would be pitted against other top teams in the first two rounds, Butler lashed out, vowing, "I'm not going to bring my team back to this tournament ever again!" Fortunately, Butler's anger eventually subsided: his "never again" vow only lasted three years.

Since Victor Valley had been eliminated in two games they had a couple of extra days to enjoy the New Year's holidays. Butler was so steamed he gave them the rest of the week off from practice. Perhaps some of the players watched the first ever Holiday Bowl in San Diego which featured Jim McMahon's Brigham Young University against Navy. Like Butler's squad, McMahon and BYU also suffered an upsetting loss.

After the holidays came league play, but the San Andreas League had a couple of twists in it this year. First, Arlington replaced Norte Vista; and, second, and much more significant, Moreno Valley and La Sierra were picked to vie for the league title rather than Victor Valley. Victor Valley was picked to finish fourth after losing four starters to graduation. Little did the prognosticators know that sophomores Taylor Conlon and Jeff Oldfield were a tandem of scorers equal to any Butler had ever had at Victor Valley. Even he didn't know how good they would turn out to be.

Anyway, Butler enjoyed the change of pace. After so many years at VVHS he could almost predict who the Rabbits would beat, who would give them a game, and who they would probably lose to. Being the underdog would make it interesting. Besides, like his mentor John Wooden, Butler knew that pre-season polls were no more than opinions. He never heeded them when Victor Valley was ranked high and he equally disregarded them this year when they were ranked low. His three season goals remained focused: win the league, win 20 games, and go to the playoffs and win the first round.

Basketball is an indoor game in which the weather is not part of the equation, unlike football and baseball, but this year the weather had a big impact on the Jackrabbits. For the first time ever at VVHS, two league games were scheduled before Christmas break but they had to be postponed because of the worst snows recorded in Victor Valley history. The Cajon pass, linking the high desert and the Inland Empire, was shut down twice, making it necessary to reschedule both the games in January. When the games were made up, they were squeezed in on days when practice normally took place giving no time to prepare the team properly. Victor Valley lost both back-to-back snowstorm makeup games to La Sierra and Moreno Valley. And losing to Moreno Valley was devastating as it marked the first time in five years that Victor Valley had lost a home league game. It looked like the prognosticators were going to be right this year.

However, in a reversal of fortune that only the makers of the movie about Claus von Bulow could appreciate more than Butler, the Rabbits rebounded from those two losses and swept through league play without another, avenging both losses to La Sierra and Moreno Valley in the mean time, and ending up as co-champs with Moreno Valley at 12-2. By virtue of a coin flip, they represented the San Andreas League as the number one team, which placed them against a number two team in the first round of the playoffs, Palo Verde, from the Imperial Valley League.

The playoff brackets looked a lot fairer to Butler than did the bracketings at the San Bernardino Kiwanis Tournament that year. Even so, in the first round against Palo Verde, Victor Valley struggled through the first three quarters, before managing to pull away in the fourth to win 72-61. Butler felt his players took the Yellowjackets too lightly and warned them there was no place for overconfidence in the playoffs.

Their second round game was on the road against El Monte, near Los Angles. Had a controversial decision not gone against Victor Valley, perhaps things might have turned out different. Near the end of the first half, Jackrabbit center, six foot seven inch Danny Kurtz, and El Monte center, Ray McNeill, were both ejected after scuffling over a loose ball. Butler was mad as hell but at least there was equity in the decision, that is until the referees held a mid-court conference and reversed themselves, deciding to reinstate McNeill. Butler went ballistic. Without his big man to neutralize McNeill the Rabbits were in big trouble. In the second half, without Kurtz, the Rabbits got no second or third shots because Kurtz couldn't get any offensive rebounds sitting in the locker room. Victor Valley lost 54-44. Butler termed it "a bad ending to a good season." And unlike the previous season's final game when Butler came away praising the officials at the Long Beach Arena, this year he was chapped that an unconscionable call had sorely affected the game's outcome.

Still, Butler was an icon in Southern California basketball circles, whether he agreed with the officials or not. Mike Kapusta, sports editor for *The Daily Press*, began calling Butler "the Wizard of the High Desert" about this time, an allusion to Butler's mentor John Wooden, the Wizard of Westwood. Like Wooden, who had since retired in 1975, Butler kept on developing fundamentally sound winning teams year in and year out. Perhaps Kapusta exaggerated when he said, "Butler continues to churn out winning basketball teams faster than Detroit can manufacture cars." The hyperbole seemed well deserved in Butler's case; after all, he'd just taken a team picked to finish fourth in league to the co-championship, picking up his sixth league championship in as many years.

Butler had scheduled the 1979-80 season to begin with a scrimmage against defending Citrus Belt League champion, 4A powerhouse Eisenhower of Rialto. Whenever possible, Butler wanted to play the biggest and the best in order to prepare his team for league. He measured his own coaching skill in these match-ups against much bigger schools. Obviously, his coaching made the difference. In 28 years Victor Valley won far more games than they lost against the bigger schools, as was the case this year when they beat the Eagles 80-63.

Butler had seven returning lettermen this year in: Taylor Conlon, Jeff Oldfield, Danny Kurtz, Guy Hunter, Carlos Jones, Pat Fealy and Billy Robinson. Transferring in from Apple Valley and New York were Eric Brown and Duane Butler. Up from the JV team were: Phil Shroyer, Kevin Vail, Keith Mason, and Aaron Potter. They would be complimented by a promising sophomore: Clyde Rivers.

Ever since Butler moved up Clifford Boyd to the varsity as a sophomore in 1973-74, he had done a better job of balancing youth with experience. He regularly scouted the junior high ninth grade teams for up and coming players who might help the varsity as sophomores, something he didn't do as much of as a younger coach. Butler was looking forward to bringing up Rivers as he had Robinson, Conlon and Oldfield the year before. They were the kind of athletes he knew he could develop into great players. (Oddly, when Victor Valley became a four year high school in the mid-eighties, Butler never brought up a freshman.)

Victor Valley won their first four games in pre-league play before losing a third round battle to the Notre Dame Knights of Sherman Oaks 59-46 in the Glendora Tournament, though they recovered quickly to trounce Garey 88-56 and take the third place trophy. Steve Scoggin was now the head coach at Glendora and had personally telephoned Butler to invite his team to the tournament. This tournament took the place of the Victorville Kiwanis Tournament that Butler decided to cancel after three years.

Without the San Bernardino Kiwanis Classic to attend the Jackrabbits had only two other December games to play, one against the Fella Scoggin led alumni (whom they shellacked 95-63), and the other against a new 3A school, Upland (whom they also handled pretty easily 70-49).

Their abbreviated pre-season saw them arrive at their league opener with a 7-1 overall record. Butler hated playing so few December games and began having second thoughts about blowing off the San Bernardino Kiwanis Classic.

In January, the Rabbits won their first eight league games and set another school record by defeating their opponents, up to that point, by an average of 37 points per game. Butler confessed that "the league was terrible other than Moreno Valley," and in their next game, Moreno Valley made good on Butler's remarks by beating the Rabbits 61-60 in Moreno Valley, snapping the Rabbits' 11 game winning streak and tying the two teams for first place.

Victor Valley won their last five league games by the same 37 points per game margin as they did the first eight but Moreno Valley won the rest of their games too, giving the Rabbits another tie for the league title with Moreno Valley who had an identical 13-1 record. This made it seven titles in a row for Butler. And just like the previous season Victor Valley won the coin flip determining who would represent the league as the number one team. This time Butler's Irish luck earned them a first round game against a number two team from the Valle Vista League.

At 21-2, the Rabbits were seeded number two in CIF 2A. In the first round they dispatched Northview handily 75-56, then edged their former Golden League rival, Ridgecrest 56-55, at a neutral court in Apple Valley. In the quarterfinals they faced Nogales, who the scouting report said were sloppy and undisciplined, two characteristics never uttered about any Butler coached team. It was true about Nogales. The Rabbits handled them 74-56, which brought the Rabbits to the semifinals again at the Long Beach Arena. If they could just get by the Mission Viejo Diablos, Butler would have another shot at winning a CIF title. Unfortunately, according to Butler, "Mission Viejo was the better team." They outlasted Victor Valley to win 63-54.

Although Butler's star players had given him some grief earlier in the year—dissension due to the backup players playing as much as the starters because Victor Valley kept blistering teams by 37 points per game—Butler was proud of how they had put their petty selfishness behind them for the good of the team and accomplished all they had. They finished 24-3. Four of five starters made All-League, and the fifth starter was named Honorable

Mention. When it was all over and the last loss of the season digested, Butler's humorous affection for his players emerged in a final newspaper quote, "I could kiss every one of them even though they are all as ugly as hell."

The 1970's had been very good to Butler and he had proven to the Southern California high school basketball community that his program was one to be reckoned with. In 18 years in Victorville he had earned a reputation as an outstanding teacher of the game to go along with his sideline reputation for being vocal, irrepressible and often bombastic toward referees. Opponents knew whenever they played Victor Valley, the Rabbits would be disciplined, fundamental and intense. They also knew the Rabbits expected to win every game they played.

With all that, you would think Butler would have silenced any critics. Not so. Aside from opposing teams' fans, who sometimes thought the Rabbits ran up the score, there were parents of his own players who didn't quite understand Butler's single-mindedness when it came to winning. For instance, in "slop-time," (when deep bench players—namely the third string—would get in to mop up during a blow out), Butler coached just as fiercely as he did with the game on the line. He got mad at players who played selfishly—trying to score so they'd get their name in the paper—or at those who didn't play hard defense because the Rabbits were so far ahead. True basketball fans understood why Butler would call a time out and vehemently chew out a third stringer who wasn't giving an optimum effort, but uninformed fans, namely parents—often parents of the third stringers—frequently misunderstood Butler as being overzealous, perhaps even fanatical. They criticized him for being so exacting of his players when they were up by 20, 30, or even 40 points.

Butler had too much pride in his program though. It didn't matter who was in the game, whether it was the first team or the last team or whether it was the JV or the sophomore level; Butler never wanted his players to look ragged, lazy, or selfish. To his critics his response was always the same: "People don't understand why I get so upset when we are ahead by so much, but I want the players to play as well as they can all the time. In a close game it makes a difference. I always want them to play as if the game is on the line. That's what develops mental toughness."

Fortunately, college recruiters were never uniformed fans. When they looked to recruit athletes for their programs, they turned first to the respected high school programs that regularly turned out athletes well-schooled in the fundamentals. Butler's Victor Valley Jackrabbits were one of the programs at the top of college recruiters' lists. Billy Robinson, who could have played college basketball but elected to play football instead (for Arizona State), found out just how widely respected Butler's program was.

"I walked into the Arizona State gym my freshman year," Robinson said, "wearing a Victor Valley basketball shirt. I just wanted to shoot around with some of the basketball players. An assistant coach saw my shirt and asked me about Butler. I was shocked. How did he know about Butler in Arizona? Then the coach told his players to watch out for me, saying if I played for Butler then I could play."

Fortunately, Butler's critics were few. He had far more supporters. Bill Lusk, a businessman whose wife Lorna was friends with Sharon Butler, became acquainted with Ollie Butler in the early Seventies. Although he didn't have children in high school, he attended VVHS basketball games between 1972-78 as his friendship with Butler grew. He admired the way Butler demanded so much from his players. Says Lusk: "Butler expected high performances from his players and he got them. I think his players were surprised at what they were able to achieve. He got more out of them than they knew they were able to give. He was a disciplinarian who taught his players how to perform under pressure. I always respected that about him. There were a few of us who went to all the games back then. We thought Butler was terrific!"

Another supporter is Pat Douglass, whom I mentioned earlier. Not only is Douglass an NCAA Division I coach and recruiter, he's also a great basketball mind who knows what it takes to build a competitive program. Like Butler, Douglass had been a winner everywhere he's coached, and knows what it takes to build and maintain winning traditions. According to Douglass, in all his years in the game—which have been primarily at the collegiate level—"Butler is the only other coach I've known whose passion for basketball rivals my own." Douglass also credits Butler with metaphorically bringing basketball to the High Desert. "Butler put in the time in the summer to keep the gym open. He took players down the hill to compete in AAU ball at Cal State Los Angeles. He inspired kids to love athletics by taking players to see Laker and Dodger games. Instead of taking a summer job like lots of teachers do to make money, Butler spent his own money on his players. He made lots of sacrifices to build his program. He had pride in his program."

By the end of the Seventies, Butler had built quite a legacy. His program was known to every major college coach in California as well as to college coaches in neighboring western states. He had sent numerous Victor Valley players on to play college basketball. Many of them had gone into teaching and coaching afterward because of his influence. He was respected and revered for his teaching of the game's fundamental skills, for his ability to motivate his players, and for his chess-like acumen at out-strategizing most opposing coaches. In winning or tying for the league title the last seven years in a row, Butler had developed a minor dynasty. He was known as a winner. He always put on a great show. He was the best kind of character actor, the kind of guy who lives the role he plays. In Victorville, Butler was loved.

To refresh you on what was going on as the Eighties got off and running let's revisit Memory Lane for a moment. Butler would be dealing with these current events in his history class at the time. This is also the backdrop to the Jackrabbits beginning the 1980-81 season.

In November of 1980, Americans selected another showman, actor and former California governor, Ronald Reagan, to become the 40th President of the United States. Like Butler, Reagan would have to deal with some baffling opponents. His first battle would be with Iran. Just after Reagan's election, 52 U. S. hostages suffered through their second Thanksgiving in Iran, where they had been forcibly detained since they were seized on Nov. 4, 1979 by militant students. Then president Jimmy Carter was ineffectual at securing the hostages' release, but after Reagan's inauguration the hostages would return home after 444 days in captivity, and Reagan would begin his administration as a bigger hero than any he had played on the silver screen.

In New York City, British pop-rocker John Lennon, was assassinated by an insane Mark Chapman, who thought this would somehow impress the actress Jody Foster. Chapman carried in his pocket a copy of J. D. Salinger's *The Catcher in the Rye*, a story about teenage disillusionment and a descent into insanity.

Closer to home, Steve Howe, a relief pitcher for Butler's favorite baseball team, the Los Angeles Dodgers, was named the National Baseball League's Rookie of the Year following a season of record setting saves.

In Victorville, the local paper was also making news to begin the Eighties. The *Daily Press* finally hired a female sportswriter, Cheryl Charles. Charles was baptized by her editor by being assigned to do the standard preseason interview with Butler, who, surprisingly, was not picking one of the schools from the city to give his team their best competition for the San Andreas League title; instead, he was picking an old rival. "I look for Barstow to be our toughest league opponent," Butler told Charles. Thus began Butler's last decade in high school basketball.

The 1980-81 Jackrabbits may have had the most talent of any one team Butler ever had. Three players off that squad would go on to play NCAA Division I college ball. Taylor Conlon got a scholarship to Dartmouth. Clyde Rivers went to Utah. And Billy Robinson went to Arizona State (although he played football rather than basketball, though most think that he could have played both the way Ronnie Lott did one year at USC). The rest of the Rabbits that year were no slouches either. They were: Dennis Cal, Jose Snoddy, Ronnie Reddick, Tim DeJarnette, Mitch Bryan, Rodney McNeil, Kevin Vail, Andy Wiggins, and Justin Skelton. This team gave Butler his best start ever. They did what no Jackrabbit team had ever done before.

In pre-league play the Rabbits went 8-0 and captured the championship of the only tournament they entered, the Glendora Tournament, beating host Glendora 49-45. Both Clyde Rivers and Billy Robinson made All-Tournament.

In league play, the Jackrabbits continued their fast and furious start by racing past each opponent, winning all their 14 games by an average of 20 points per game. At 22-0, they were ranked number one in CIF and almost assured to go to the finals and win it all. Never before had a Butler team entered the CIF playoffs undefeated.

In the first round of the playoffs, the Rabbits were rattled by the Covina Colts. Although the Rabbits won 45-41, their confidence was shaken. Covina wasn't supposed to be that strong, they were only a third place team.

Then in the second round, Victor Valley was re-matched with the Burros of Ridgecrest, an old nemesis and the team they had knocked off last year by two points in the quarterfinals. Ridgecrest had another great team and was bent on revenge. Butler knew they would be tough to beat in Trona, the neutral site Burros had picked to play in. He was right. The Rabbits had a cold shooting night and Taylor Conlon and Billy Robinson were forced to the bench for much of the game because of foul trouble. In an even tighter game than last year's two point win, the Rabbits were undone, coming out on the other end this time, losing 60-61.

It didn't matter that everyone on this team had made school history by winning 23 straight games. It didn't matter that as a junior Jose Snoddy set a new school single season assist record with 165 in 24 games. It didn't matter that the Jackrabbits had just won their eighth league title in a row. It didn't matter that Victor Valley was ranked number one in CIF virtually all season long and picked to cruise to the championship. It didn't matter that Conlan and Robinson were both expected to get Division I scholarships. It didn't matter that Butler had proven to everyone involved in Southern California that he was one of the best high school basketball coaches of all time. What mattered was, at 23-1, the Rabbits were ending the season as losers, a chronic pill that Butler kept having to swallow. He could only shake his head. What kind of a destiny was this? A backup player offered the only logical explanation: "It was the sulfur."

There is a strong sulfur smell permeating the air in Trona that comes from the mining operations. To denizens of Trona it is the smell of money, as practically everyone in town works at the mines, but to visitors it just smells like rotten eggs. It is known to give out-of-towners headaches. The Rabbits left Trona with a big headache.

In 1981-82, with Robinson and Conlon packed off to college, Clyde Rivers still had another season to go at Victor Valley. In two previous years on the varsity he had affectionately earned two nicknames for the way he moved up and down the court: "Clyde the Glide" and "Scooty." As a senior, Rivers was a man on a mission. Victor Valley had produced some top college recruits in the past few years and he wanted to be sure and join those ranks. As a junior he'd begun receiving recruiting letters from colleges. What he needed now was a big senior year to get him into a major college program. So when he scored 37 points to lead the Jackrabbits to a 91-90 win in the opening game of the season against the alumni, he got off to a great start.

The Jackrabbits again had a roster full of returners. Back were: Jose Snoddy, Mitch Bryan, Dennis Cal, Andy Wiggins and Rodney McNeil; plus the usual guys moving up in the program: Willie Walker, Dwight McElroy, Mike Holland, Danny Escobedo, Dave Spaugy, Billy Hart, Harold Colvin and Moses Green.

Victor Valley had a good pre-league showing, though not quite as impressive as their undefeated month of December last year. They went 8-3, and much to Steve Scoggin's chagrin the Jackrabbits again beat his Glendora Tartans in the Glendora Tournament, though this time it was for the Consolation Championship. Unfortunately, the Rabbits entered league play on a losing note, dropping a tight pre-league contest to Reggie Miller's Riverside Poly Bears—though they fared a lot better than the Lady Jackrabbits, who allowed Reggie's sister Cheryl to single- handedly dismantle them in Victorville when she scored 52 points and pulled down 39 rebounds. No wonder she was a four-time high school All-American.

The good news about the loss to Riverside was that the boys got losing out of their system for a while and breezed through league play 10-0 in the newly reconfigured smaller San Andreas League. This gave Butler 31 straight league wins and his ninth consecutive league title. Rivers achieved his goal of generating serious interest among major colleges. He averaged 30 points per game and more than 50 NCAA Division I schools tried to recruit him.

Butler's players weren't the only ones being recruited by colleges, he was also being encouraged to move up to the collegiate level. A number of programs wanted him, from the community college ranks, through the NAIA schools, all the way up to the NCAA Division I schools. But Butler had long ago decided that high school coaching was his niche. With the long distance travel, the weekly schmoozing of the alumni and administration and the public speaking engagements required of college coaches, he'd have no time for family each night. Unknown to many fans, this was where Butler drew his strength, from the sanctuary of his home and his supportive wife. Besides, Butler had a more important goal in mind. His son Mike would be entering high school in 1987. Having his son play high school ball for him was better than any college job that he might be offered.

The Rabbits entered the CIF playoffs at 18-3 and ranked number two. Butler liked this. He never liked being ranked number one. "There's something about being number one that makes your opponents try harder," he lamented, remembering last year's quarterfinal's loss when they were undefeated and ranked number one.

Unfortunately, their number two ranking only got them one round further than their number one ranking did the year before. They beat the Ganesha Giants 96-75 in the first round, then edged the Indio Rajahs 81-77 in the second round, but were foiled in the quarterfinals, this time by the La Habra Highlanders 72-66. They finished 20-4, again giving Butler the three benchmarks he measured each season by: to win league, win 20 games and advance past the first round of the playoffs. Besides those annual goals, Butler had also put together an amazing 174-35 record in winning nine straight league crowns between 1974 and 1982. No wonder he was receiving weekly letters and phone calls from college athletic directors, not to mention the occasional knock on the door from an occasional university president. But like all good things, inevitably this string of league titles had to come to an end.

1982-83 would bring Butler's reign of championships to a close. In pre-league play the Jackrabbits were a disappointment, giving notice around the Inland Empire that Victor Valley might have some chinks in their armor this year. They did, the biggest chink being the broken foot of point guard Dennis Cal, who'd injured it in football—one reason why Butler preferred his basketball players not to play football. Without Cal in the line-up the Rabbits went 2-6 in their first eight games. However, when Cal returned in late December to play in his first game of the season, he scored 28 points and Butler was sure the tide was ready to turn even though the Rabbits lost the game badly to Riverside Poly 63-86 and were now a dismal 2-7 prior to beginning league.

Joining Cal this year on the roster were mostly inexperienced underclassmen and a couple of seniors who'd never played varsity before. The roster was made up of: Dennis Cal, Andy Gowell, Mike Morales, Kurt

Story, Tony Miller, Joey Reyes, Darrel Langlois, Tim Williams, Derek Allen, Guy Johnson, Jimmy Coomes, and Mike Davis.

With Cal back to run the offense the Rabbits would win the SAL title one last time, though not with the convincing undefeated league record they'd achieved in a number of prior seasons; nor would they win the title outright, they would again share it, this time with Barstow who had an identical 8-2 record. Victor Valley would again go to the playoffs as the first place team from the league, but not because they won another coin flip; even though they tied with Barstow for first place, they were the champs because they had beaten Barstow both times they played them. Victor Valley's two losses came to cross-town rival Apple Valley, in double-overtime, 48-52, and to San Bernardino 56-61. The eight games they won were all close, too, under 10 points per game, unlike the past few years where they'd blown by most teams with big margins.

As the first place team from the San Andreas League, VVHS drew a home game in the first round of the CIF playoffs and used the home court to advantage in cruising by the Coachella Valley Arabs 71-50. In the second round though, the Rabbits didn't have enough scoring punch or rebounding strength to stave off the Workman Lobos from the City of Industry, losing a tough game 51-56. Was Butler down on this squad or himself after a lowly 12-9 season? How could he be? They'd achieved two of his three yearly goals, and considering the reversal this team had made after their slow start, Butler felt they deserved more praise than did many of his teams to whom success came easier. "I have absolutely no complaints," Butler told *Daily Press* reporter Cheryl Charles. "We didn't play bad at all, we just got beat on the boards. That's been our weakness all season." Workman's six foot seven inch phenomenon, Vincent Blow, had scored 28 points and dominated the boards in exploiting that yearlong weakness.

In 22 years at VVHS Butler was already a legend. His record at VVHS stood at 401-152. He was an old hand at the game, confident in his abilities, not prone to worrying. So when his Jackrabbits were picked to finish in the middle of the league pack, maybe no higher than third, he shook it off and challenged his team to work harder this year to prove the critics wrong. San Bernardino High School, under their new coach Scott Kay, was predicted to win the league. This didn't bother Butler a bit. He remembered what happened the last time the Rabbits were picked to finish poorly, they tied for the title. Unfortunately, this year Butler's confidence couldn't carry a thoroughly inconsistent squad.

In 1983-84 the Rabbits were led by three returners who'd seen a lot of action the year before: Kurt Story, Mike Morales and Mike Stewart. Also back were: Andy Gowell, Tony Evans, Tony Miler, Guy Johnson, and Tim

Ribbons. To these letterman Butler added five guys from the JV and sophomore teams: Richard Blais, Oki Bennet, Al Carlucci, Kevin Malcolm, Richard Mosely, plus two transfers, Sean Bazille and Ron Silver.

The Rabbits started slow but nothing like the year before, going a respectable 8-6 in pre-league games. Butler called them his "Jekyll and Hyde team." They'd win one then lose one, win one and lose one. They'd play great and Butler couldn't praise them enough, then they'd play like they'd never been taught anything fundamental at all. In the Glendora Tournament, they won their first game then lost the next two.

Butler, too, showed a little Jekyll and Hyde. His "never again" boycott of the San Bernardino Kiwanis Classic came to an end after three years. He swallowed his pride and sent in the registration fee, reversing himself because he felt he was hurting his team by keeping them out of the biggest tournament in the area. I remember my dad used to always say, "It takes a big man to admit when he is wrong." Butler's decision to rejoin the tournament was tantamount to that.

In the Kiwanis Classic, the Rabbits reversed what they did at Glendora. They lost their first game and were dropped to the consolation bracket, where they won the rest and took home the Consolation Championship trophy. Butler hoped this would jump start the Rabbits and get them over their win one lose one hump; however, as it turned out, those three wins in a row, their longest winning streak of the season, would turn out to be their only stretch of straight track in a winding, curving, topsy-turvy season.

As soon as league play began VVHS returned to the ups and downs of their roller coaster ways. They won two, then lost two, won one, lost two more, then won again, before losing their last two and ending up 4-6 in league to finish fourth—right in the middle as had been predicted. What hurt worse was they lost to Apple Valley for the second year in a row, giving Butler his third loss against them in his career. Butler hated to lose to Apple Valley. The Rabbits also missed the playoffs for the first time since 1972.

Yet here's what Butler had to say when the season ended. No sour grapes, no pointing the finger in other directions, just a simple assessment of their weaknesses and what he expected for next year: "We're as good a team as anyone in this league, but we've been plagued by no rebounding and poor baseline defense. We'll be back. I was pleased with the play of the young guys. We'll just start over again next year." That was Butler for you, ever the optimist. No little thing like a fourth place finish after 10 straight championships was going to get him down.

Butler began the 1984-85 season reflectively, mulling over last year's break-even 12-12 season. He wanted his team to get back to their characteristic quickness, something he felt they were missing last year. What kind of Jackrabbits weren't quick? He also wanted to pick up the intensity level. Last year's team was too passive. Butler didn't blame his players though, he blamed himself. "I took a lot of things for granted the last few years and eased up on the players." This year that wouldn't happen.

To add to the pressure of returning the Rabbits to prominence, Butler's fellow teachers went out on strike just as basketball season was getting under way and of course they wanted him to join them. While Butler professed strong union loyalty and solidarity with his fellow teachers' grievances, he couldn't see abandoning three levels of basketball players who would be devastated if their season fell through. Butler had four players on this team that had the potential go on to play college ball if they made a good showing this year. Without him to guide the Rabbits those dreams would not materialize. He couldn't let the players down, so Butler told his assistant coaches that he would coach all three levels while they were out on strike and he continued to work, much to the annoyance of many newer teachers who didn't understand his loyalty to the kids. "I'd be out carrying the biggest picket sign they could give me," Butler lamented, "if it weren't for my players. In spirit though, I'm out there with them on strike."

Mike Stewart was the captain of the team and Butler expected him to instill a fierce desire to win in his teammates. Also back were: Tony Evans, Tony Miller, Oki Bennet and Richard Mosely. The newcomers were: Bob Dwyer, Scott Willey, Wilson Guitterres, Randy Alex, Jimmy Armstrong, Adrian Crumb, Mark Cordero, David Roark and Joey Reyes.

Mediocrely, the Rabbits stumbled through pre-league play much the way they did the previous year and Butler had to have another talk with his team captain. They went 4-4, though the good news was they finally defeated Riverside Poly 66-58 after falling to them two years in a row. This was a milestone game, giving Butler his 500th career win, a goal he had set for himself in 1956. Unfortunately, this career high was followed by a disappointing league-opening loss to Apple Valley, Butler's third loss to them in three years, though only his fourth loss to them in 16 years. Fortunately, this would be the last time Butler ever lost to Apple Valley. Why had VVHS lost again for the third time in three years to a team they'd always dominated? Simple. "Poor defense," Butler pointed out. "We couldn't have guarded a $10 bill if it was lying on the floor."

In spite of their league-opening loss, the Rabbits did get back to their characteristic quickness and intensity, going 10-4 in league and tying with Apple Valley for second place. In the playoffs however, Victor Valley went as the third place team which forced them to face the Valle Vista League champion, Edgewood of Covina, who nipped the Rabbits 65-61 in the first round to end their year with a 14-8 overall record.

In vogue to begin the 1985-86 season was the personal computer. It was tabbed as the latest time saving device to make family record keeping easy and manageable. Databases could be loaded with essential family information, providing fingertip accessibility for keeping track of personal finances, medical histories, mailing lists, pantry stock and just about anything else you could name having to do with domestic living. Even coaches were intrigued by this innovative technology.

Statistics are a coach's primary motivational tool. Every player wants to know how many points he's scored, rebounds he's pulled down, steals he's made, and so forth, and how the numbers are adding up over the season. Coaches are responsible for keeping accurate tabs in many different categories. Coaches use these numbers to challenge their players to exceed themselves. These statistics are also vital to local news agencies, college recruiters and regional sports associations like the CIF. So when the computer became affordable for the average person, coaches were some of the first in line to get one.

Not Ollie Butler. He continued to tally his statistics the old-fashioned way, by hand, with a pencil. Though he always had a trained cadre of student-statisticians to tally the game numbers (his three daughters were his favorites since they were the easiest to get a hold of if he had a question), he was the one who calculated the field stats and totaled them up when he got home at night. Sure, a computer might be faster, less inclined to make a mathematic error, and more reliable late at night after a gut-wrenching loss, but Butler wasn't about to relinquish one of his favorite coaching responsibilities to a machine. *Might as well let a machine do the coaching too.*

Besides the novelty of the computer, there was another innovation going on in the world of basketball as Butler began his 24th season at VVHS, another rule change, a modification of the 1977-78 rule governing coaches sideline gamesmanship. Instigated locally by the CIF, the new rule inhibited the coach's movement even more than the last six point rule had. The rule stated the coach must stay seated the entire game. I heard from three different sources the rumor that the rule came about due to Butler's increasing run-ins with substandard officials. Butler was known to glare menacingly, bark argumentatively and to wag his index finger disapprovingly at officials the same way he did his players if he felt they had made a mistake. I don't know if there is any truth to the rumor that this change was also stealthily called the "Butler Rule" behind closed doors at CIF headquarters, I'm just passing along what I heard.

When asked what he thought about it, Butler offered a typical understatement, "I don't care for it much." He hoped the rule wouldn't last (it didn't), and that they'd eventually go to a coach's boxed area where a coach would have the latitude to stand up and move around a bit if he wanted to (this is exactly what happened with the next rule shift).

This year Butler had an overflow of talented returners plus a promising group of underclassmen moving up to the varsity. The roster consisted of: All-CIF football wide-receiver Steve Clay (who was late coming out because his football team had gone to the CIF finals), Tony Evans, Tony Miller, Bob Dwyer, Mark Cordero, Joey Reyes, Jimmy Armstrong, Greg Hartle, Andre Burkes, Ike Jackson, Mark Height, Mark Seals, Chris Frasier and transfer Bruce Prey.

The Rabbits opened the year in a new venue when they were invited to play in the Yucaipa Tip-Off Classic. Their first year in the tournament they won it by decisively upending the defending champion Cajon 66-42, after rolling over Rim of the World and Ontario in the first two rounds of the eight team tournament. This was to become a minor tradition for Victor Valley, who would win the Yucaipa tournament three more years in a row, However, when Victor Valley's reign came to an end with a loss to Cajon in the finals in 1989, the loss would turn out to be tragic in scope, extending beyond the game, the season and Ollie Butler's legendary career. It would send shock waves through Southern California high school basketball and create a scandal that would devastate both Butler and his son Mike. But I better not get ahead of myself.

After the Yucaipa Classic, VVHS took a turn for the worse, losing their first two games in the Moreno Valley Tournament—to Indio and Redlands. Their record stood at 3-2, and for the next month the Rabbits had a hard time finding their rhythm.

On December 17, they won their league opener against La Sierra but in their rematch with Cajon a couple of days later—the same team they had easily spanked in the Yucaipa Classic finals—they were out-played. Cajon's six foot five inch, Julius Davison, scored 34 points, and his six foot seven inch counterpart, Melvin Love, added 23. And it got worse before it got better when two humbling losses and an early exit from the San Bernardino Kiwanis Classic forced the Rabbits to reexamine their work ethic. In the Kiwanis Classic they lost first to Redlands, who had beaten them at Moreno Valley already, and then to Hesperia, their first loss ever to the newest high school in the High Desert.

After the holidays VVHS rebounded to win two games against Apple Valley and Norte Vista, but when they played Jerry Bunch's Hesperia Scorpions for the second time, they got stung again. In a furious attempt to evoke some emotion from his stoic upperclassmen, Butler lambasted his veterans for a "lack of senior leadership." Did his tirade have the desired effect? For one game it did, they smoked Barstow by 20 in their next outing, but when they went up against CIF number one ranked San Bernardino, no amount of senior leadership could keep them from getting pummeled on the Cardinals' home court 82-55.

When they began the second round of league play, it looked like there might be a déjà vu thing going on. They again beat La Sierra but were in turn beaten by Cajon, and at 5-4 in league and 8-8 overall, they seemed destined to watch the playoffs from the stands when league wrapped up. Butler got in their faces and challenged them, "We aren't going to see any post-season play at all if you guys can't stop this win one and lose one syndrome."

Butler's warning worked better this time, the Rabbits responded with five straight wins, upsetting the number one ranked Cardinals in the process. Butler called this "slaying Goliath." San Bernardino was bigger, faster and more athletic, yet under Butler's wily guidance, the Rabbits exploited every Cardinal weakness. (San Bernardino coach Scott Kay would grow tired of this familiar refrain. During his glory years at San Bernardino, when they were winning the league year in and year out behind superstar Bryon Russell and Victor Valley was coming in second place, their perfect league record was usually marred by one loss—to Victor Valley in the Keith Gunn gym. And even when San Bernardino did go 14-0 in league and swept to the CIF Championship with an undefeated record, Victor Valley held the Cardinals to 43 points, and Russell to 12 points, losing to them by 7, the closest game San Bernardino had all year).

Victor Valley finished league with a 10-4 record and a third place finish, just squeaking them into the playoffs with a wild-card berth. They drew Rim of the World and defeated them handily 68-47 but in the next round against Rio Hondo League Champion, the Blair Vikings, VVHS folded their season 53-69. They finished a decent 14-9 and in bowing out of the playoffs early Butler found refuge in his statistics, announcing that Mark Cordero had set a new school free-throw shooting percentage record, besting by three percent Sergio Lugo's nine year old record of 84 percent. Statistics were Butler's silver lining in every cloudy season.

In all of Butler's years of teaching and coaching, the 1986-87 season was the hardest for him to get through and if it weren't for basketball, he may not have survived it. You will remember that prior to the 1963-64 season Butler cried in front of his students when John F, Kennedy was assassinated. This season he cried again, tears that periodically still flow. Prior to the season, Ollie and Sharon's middle daughter, Rebecca Ann, was tragically killed in an automobile accident.

Willie McDonald, Butler's assistant coach and close friend, said, "Becky's death was unbelievably hard on Ollie and Sharon but they held up strongly during that devastating time." At school, students and players asked McDonald what they should say to Mr. Butler. McDonald wondered himself what could possibly be said to console a grieving parent who had lost one of his most precious treasures. He was having trouble himself finding the right words. Butler's students and players were heartbroken for him and wanted to show their sympathy.

"Fortunately," McDonald said, "Ollie made it easy on everyone. One day he began class by thanking his students for their concern, then asked them not to say anything more about it. He preferred to mourn privately, the less said the better." That's how Ollie Butler still feels today, although with the passage of time he's gotten more comfortable about being able to reminisce with friends about Becky's life without breaking down.

When the season came around, Butler was grateful. Losing himself in the distraction of basketball was just what he needed, and for the first time in a long time Butler saw basketball in a new light. He had an epiphany in realizing his job was really all about the people involved. Over the years, he had to admit, he'd gotten caught up in the wins, the success and the egotism of it all. He knew he was a good teacher and a good coach. He was proud of his work ethic and the success that came as a result. It was a shame, he thought, that it took Becky's death to remind him that basketball was just a game and that the most important part wasn't winning or losing, it was the opportunity to work with the people playing that was most important. Strange how tragedy sometimes opens our eyes to things we should have always seen and known.

The Jackrabbits came out of the blocks racing under the newly enlightened Butler. They won their first three in a row and repeated as champs of the Yucaipa Tip-Off Classic. Then they won two more in the Riverside Tournament (held at Moreno Valley) to make it into the finals. But against host Moreno Valley, the Rabbits got drilled 77-51 and had to settle for the second place trophy. Butler commented afterwards, "We are a good team, but tonight we got beat by a better team."

In a trend that developed in the mid-Eighties, the Rabbits no longer had a distinct pre-league season any more. In early December they played six tournament games, then began league play with two games just before Christmas break. (They lost to Bryon Russell's San Bernardino led Cardinals by 20 points but rebounded from that loss and beat Cajon by an equal margin.) Then it was time to go back to non-league tournament play in the San Bernardino Kiwanis Classic. (They won their first game but lost the next two and were out in three.) In the old days there was always a distinct preseason of 10 or so non-league games before league play began. Butler liked that arrangement as it prepared his team for league. But even though this new trend was interruptive, it didn't upset Butler the same way it might have in the past. These were all minor details to the newly enlightened Butler. They didn't matter at all.

When league play resumed in January after the holidays, the Rabbits ran off five straight wins to complete the first round of league play 6-1. Then they avenged their 20 point loss to San Bernardino by slaying Goliath at home again for the second year in a row, climbing into a tie for first place. However, they were upset by Cajon in their next game when Melvin Love erupted for 38 points, and dropped right back into second place where they remained for the duration of league play.

Thanks to unselfish team ball played by: Steve Clay, Bryan Childers, Mark Height (great name for a basketball player don't you think!), Greg Hartle, Mark Hammond, Nick Hartman, Denny Lester, Mike Wollangk, Chris Frasier, Ike Jackson, Shawn King and Paul Portis, the Rabbits didn't lose another game, finishing 12-2, one game behind San Bernardino's 13-1 record. At 18-5 overall, and having beaten number one San Bernardino, the defending CIF champs, the Rabbits entered the playoffs ranked number eight in Southern California.

By this point in the season, Steve Clay had emerged as the team's leader. A two time All-CIF wide receiver on the football team, Steve was tough, talented and determined. He wanted to be All-CIF in basketball too and so far he was having the kind of season to deserve it, but only if the Rabbits advanced far into the playoffs would he be considered.

In the first round VVHS drew a third place team from the Mission Valley League, the Rosemead Panthers, and didn't have too much trouble getting past them 65-50. In the second round they were fortunate to draw a second place team from the Desert Valley League, the Indio Rajahs. They handled the Rajahs by the same 15 points they did the Panthers in the first round, wining 69-53. *If only all the playoff games could be this close!*

But in the quarterfinals, against the league champion of the Los Padres League, they had a tough draw in the St. Joseph's Knights of Santa Maria. When teams get to the quarterfinals, the CIF, in order to make things fair and equitable, require teams to finish the playoffs by playing on neutral courts. First there is a coin flip to see which team gets the home court advantage. Whoever wins the coin toss selects a neutral court near their own school. Against St. Joseph's VVHS won the coin toss and picked Apple Valley High School to play the quarterfinal game at. Santa Maria was a long ways from Apple Valley High School, giving Victor Valley a slight edge, but St. Joseph's was so good that if Steve Clay hadn't burned the nets for 26 points and helped suppress a Knight's comeback with his football-like defense, it is unlikely the Rabbits would have eked out a 68-62 win the way they did. So in the semi-finals, when VVHS again won the coin toss, they picked Apple Valley High School one more time to give them home court advantage.

The Woodbridge Warriors, champions of the Sea View League, were favored to beat Victor Valley despite being the visitors who had a two hour bus trip from Irvine to hostile Apple Valley. They were favored mainly because they had a six foot nine inch center in Adam Keefe (who went on to play at Stanford and then went into the NBA and played for Utah). VVHS wasn't given much of a chance. That didn't set too well with Steve Clay. He had led the football team to the finals of CIF and wanted to do the same for the basketball team.

With Lute Olsen of Arizona in the stands to scout Keefe, Keefe did what he'd been doing all year. Against Victor Valley he scored a game high 34 points and pulled down 22 rebounds. No one could stop him. However, that was expected. What was unexpected was the performance of the guy who caught Olsen's attention even more than Keefe, Steve Clay. Clay was the soul of the Rabbits. Single-handedly he refused to allow the Warriors to pull away. His tenacity inspired the rest of the Rabbits to play their best game of the season. Every time Woodbridge would move out to an eight or ten point lead, Clay would lead the Rabbits back to within two, three, or four. Despite Keefe's domination, the Warriors couldn't outdistance the Rabbits. Olsen wasn't the only scout in the house, there were a number of others too, and by the end of the game most of them were talking about Clay, who had scored 29 points.

Unfortunately, it wasn't enough. Woodbridge held on at the free throw line when the Rabbits had to start fouling in the last minute to stop the clock. They hit all their free-throws and won 73-65. But Butler wasn't upset by the close loss the way he normally might have been. He was actually pretty satisfied. He hadn't expected the Rabbits to make it this far into the playoffs. The returning lettermen off last year's 14-9 team hadn't intimated they'd turn out to be this good at the beginning of the season. No one was more surprised than he was at the success of this squad. Plus, he knew he didn't start the season off with his usual enthusiasm and high hopes. There was never a thought about going to the CIF semifinals. Though more philosophical than ever when the season began, he had to admit to himself that all year long he'd used basketball as an outlet to get him through each day. His afternoon practices were the only thing that kept his mind from returning to the empty void that Becky's passing had left behind. Yet here were his boys, semifinalists, finishing the year at 21-6, giving Butler his first 20 game win season in five years. How strange it all seemed.

When asked to explain it, Butler could only figure that they had worked harder this season than they had in the recent past. Though he had put in more time and extra effort this year than ever before to keep his mind off his personal woes, he modestly attributed the success to the fact that "We had mostly young guys who over achieved." Steve Clay was the biggest of those overachievers. He was named All-CIF in basketball to go along with the same recognition he had earned in football.

Life, as I am sure you will agree, often has a mysterious rhythm of its own. The comedies and tragedies occur when you least expect them then turn on each other and become something else in ways you'd never expect though sometimes these unpredictable rhythms have a way of balancing out. For Ollie Butler, the start of the 1987-88 season was just the day-dream he needed to counter last season's surreal nightmarish beginning. Tragedy needed some comic relief and Butler sought it in his son Mike.

A vigilant varsity coach always has at least one eye on the lower levels of his program but this year Butler had both eyes wide open. His son Mike had finally arrived, a member of the freshman class of '91, and true to Butler form he tried out and made the freshman basketball team. With Mike's ascension to high school, his dad could see him more frequently and keep an eye on him. Mike, who had always been care-free, happy and full of life, was now going through something no child should have to experience, the tragic death of a beloved sister.

Butler thought Becky's death may have been harder on Mike than the rest of the family. Kids didn't understand things the way adults did and naturally had a harder time putting death in perspective. Mike's usual life-of-the-party demeanor had changed in the past year. During his eighth grade year he'd become quiet and withdrawn, his grades had dropped and he was unmotivated. His dad was concerned. He hoped he could pump a little life back into Mike, who had always loved being with his dad in the gym. Now they would be together for the next four years.

Family was everything to Butler and with his other two daughters grown and successfully working their way through college Mike was the only one at home to worry about. Butler was glad that Mike and his friends (who were like brothers to Mike and additional sons to Butler) were on campus, the next four years would be like a big family reunion. He was even hoping to have Mike and his friends as his own students. He had waited for this for so long now, it was hard to believe it was really happening. It was more important than ever too. Both father and son needed this as part of their recovery. Now all Mike had to do was keep up his studies, develop in the program, and perhaps by the time he was a junior he'd be ready for the varsity. Perhaps by then his grief would have subsided and he'd be back to his old happy-go-lucky self.

The Rabbit varsity began the season the same way it had the previous year, they went 3-0 in the Yucaipa Tip-Off Classic and won the title again. Senior Paul Portis was named the MVP, while fellow senior, Ike Jackson, was also named to the All-Tournament team. They also repeated their performance in the Riverside Tournament at Moreno Valley, winning their first two to put them in the finals, where, unfortunately, they again lost to host Moreno Valley, though this time it was a lot closer, 69-70. Paul Portis and Mark Height made the All-Tournament team.

Though they had two league games scheduled before Christmas break, they could only play one of them. They handled Hesperia 64-47, but the other game had to be postponed because of snow that made the Cajon pass impassable.

Then came the Kiwanis Classic in San Bernardino where for the third time in three tournaments VVHS made it to the finals. Unfortunately, as in Moreno Valley, they had to settle for second place, losing to the San Bernardino Cardinals who were again led by Bryon Russell. Butler was glad it was Russell's senior season at last. He'd enjoy watching Russell on TV playing for some major college a lot more than he would watching him break down his Jackrabbits as he had for four years now.

Following Christmas break, VVHS resumed league contests, and behind the experienced play of: Bryan Childers, Nick Hartman, Paul Portis, Ike Jackson and Mike Wollangk, the Rabbits went 11-3 in league. They almost finished 12-2, but their last league game ended up as buzzer-beating-punch-in-the-stomach loss, courtesy of Barstow's Eric Shibley, who hoisted a shot from afar with a second to go that sailed cleanly through the net to send VVHS into the playoffs on a losing note. The Rabbits were ranked number four in CIF before the loss to Barstow, but after the loss they dropped to number eight, which made a difference in the playoff seedings.

In the first round the Rabbits faced off against the champs of the Suburban League, the Norwalk Lancers. The scouting report showed the two teams to be about the same in size and statistics. It didn't turn out to be that way in reality. VVHS was underestimated. The Rabbits cruised by the Lancers 95-61. But in the second round the Rabbits didn't have such an easy time of it. The Montview League champs, the Duarte Falcons, were flying high on the wings of shooting guard Mario Rose and aerobatic six foot five inch forward Otis Mixon. Together they combined for nearly 40 points, giving them just enough oomph to float past the Rabbits 60-54. Of course assistant coach Sergio Lugo's second half technical foul and ejection didn't help. It created a six point swing which ended up being the difference in the game. But no one could fault Lugo, especially Butler. When it came to technical fouls, Lugo had learned from the master himself. The Rabbits finished 20-6, bringing the number of Butler's 20+ win seasons to 14 in 26 years at VVHS. This was his last 20+ game winning season. He only had two more seasons to go.

The 1988-89 season began identically to the previous three with Victor Valley taking another Yucaipa Tip-Off Classic championship. This was becoming a source of contention. The fans in Yucaipa were wondering if anyone besides VVHS would ever win their tournament. Cajon tried, giving Victor Valley a close game, but behind the play of tournament MVP, Nick Hartman, the Rabbits held off the cowboys 58-53.

Nick Hartman, Mike Wollangk, Thomas Wilkins, Jason Bragg and Carlton Hyder were the starters this year. After Yucaipa, they went 2-0 in the Moreno Valley Tournament, but did not win it when foul weather in the Cajon Pass kept them from making it down the hill to their second round game that could not be made up. (Butler would not count this as a forfeit loss. Weather was an act of God. His boys did not lose a game they did not play.) After Christmas they took the Consolation Championship in the Kiwanis Tournament with a 3-1 showing, placing both Mike Wollangk and Jason Bragg on the All-Tournament team. Then came league play.

Victor Valley lost some momentum in the beginning of January by losing two of their first four league games to Barstow and San Bernardino. This year the league had shrunk from eight teams to six so losing two in the first round didn't bode well. The second round was about identical to the first, VVHS again lost to Barstow and San Bernardino, but won their other three league games. This gave them a 6-4 record and a third place league finish, though at 18-6 they were ranked 10th in CIF going into the playoffs.

In the first round they humbled Elsinore 84-52. Unfortunately, their second round opponent, the Perris Panthers, champions of the Skyline League, gave the Rabbits an identical humbling to the one they gave Elsinore, winning by the same 84-52 score. The Rabbits finished the season 19-7.

Mike Wollangk had a terrific senior year. He was the team's leading scorer and earned a scholarship to play at the University of Alaska. Big man Nick Hartman was also graduating and going off to college. Fortunately for Butler, he had Jason Bragg coming back next year along with Carlton Hyder and Thomas Wilkins. All three had picked up valuable varsity experience and Butler was counting on their leadership. And best of all, a dream Butler had been having recurrently since his son Mike was born in 1973, was about to come true.

Mike had a pretty good freshman year, all things considered, and as a sophomore he had played well on the JV team and kept his grades up to eligibility standards. He would be ready to join the varsity next season as a junior. His spirits had improved greatly, though basketball was truly the only thing inspiring him. His grades were only adequate. He wasn't exactly losing himself in his school work. Some of his teachers told his dad that he wasn't putting enough effort into his studies. No excuses, but it was tough for algebra and geometry to matter to Mike after recently losing his sister. Still, his dad thought things were looking up and he couldn't have been happier to be realizing this long held dream. Together they would make it happen.

DAVID KNISS

END OF AN ERA

"Fellas, I think you may have sealed my fate," Butler quipped morosely as the team van chugged up the I-15 on-ramp headed toward Victorville.

It was Wednesday, December 6, 1989, and Ollie Butler was only a few games into his 28th season as head coach at Victor Valley High. In 27 previous years at VVHS, he'd taken the Rabbits to the playoffs 21 times, twice to the finals and three times to the semifinals. His top-tier high school basketball program was praised throughout Southern California. Butler was the quintessential high school coach. How could his destiny have come to this?

The hour long ride from Moreno Valley back to Victorville gave both Butler and his players time to think about what had just occurred. *Damn!* thought more than one Victor Valley player. *What the hell did we just do?* And Butler, edgily steering the van homeward, the dizzying events of the past couple of hours swirling in his head like a cyclone, was asking himself one question: *Could this be it?*

Butler had been in hot water before. Each season someone would inevitably complain about his sideline tirades and he would be called into the office by the current principal. Butler knew this passion was a double-edged sword, both a strength and a weakness. He knew that sometimes he got carried away. In fact, to keep himself in check, some years he trained the stat girls to give him a gentle reminder to simmer down if they saw him getting carried away. They would pull on Butler's shirt from behind when he got up off the bench to protest a call. Legend has it that Superintendent Harvey Irwin used to do the same thing early in Butler's career.

In 27 seasons at Victor Valley Butler had met with every reigning principal to discuss some heated exchange that had occurred at a basketball game, yet each time Butler survived the cautionary counseling, walking out with a reminder from the boss that he was an ambassador of good will for the school and that he should see to it that his temper and courtside manner did not bring reproach to the school or its administration. This had always worked, at least until the latest administration arrived. Victor Valley's newest principal was Julian Weaver. It was Weaver Butler was thinking about as he wheeled the team van home. *I'll bet Weaver will try and fire me over this.*

"I think this could be it!" someone in the front bench seat of the team van heard Butler mutter to himself.

136

Of course you want to know, *What happened?* I wish I could tell you for certain, but I wasn't there. However, I did a lot of digging around. I went back and read all the newspaper articles written about the incident. I also interviewed as many people as I could find who were directly involved. Unfortunately, some of the key people I wanted to talk with were unavailable, while others flat out refused to be interviewed. So, I want to you to know that I have taken some liberties in recreating this incident. In order to make the story flow I have created reasonable dialogue and thoughts based on the information I gathered. The events occurred 13 years ago. People's memories have faded. Truth, as you know, is bound up in perception. Everyone I spoke with involved in this altercation had a different perception. People's perceptions have changed over time. Prejudices have tainted the facts. The video-tape recording this incident is no longer extant. But according to my research, this is as close as I can get to the way it all went down.

As soon as the Jackrabbits loped into the Moreno Valley High School gymnasium to warm up for their first round game in the Riverside Tournament they knew they were in trouble.

Not these guys again.

Jeez, they killed us at Yucaipa. We won't get any calls tonight!

Two days earlier, referees Al Jury and Dick Smith (who did not return my calls when I tried to get their side of the story) had officiated the finals of the Yucaipa Tip-Off Classic between VVHS and Cajon. A questionable foul against Victor Valley, called by Jury in the waning seconds of the game, handed Cajon a couple of free throws and a 69-68 win, denying VVHS its 5th straight tournament crown. VVHS players felt strong-arm-robbed by officials who had long ago become Butler's adversaries. The players griped to Jury and Smith as the game ended but Butler shooed his players into the locker room. It was his job to handle the referees. With his players behind closed doors, Butler reeled off a few choice words to Smith and Jury about the prejudicial quality of their officiating then stalked off to the locker room himself. That was the end of it. Or at least he thought that was the end of it.

Now, here were Smith and Jury again, loosening up in front of the scorekeeper's table prior to calling the opening round game of the Riverside Tournament between VVHS and Damien High. Butler was not happy about this. *Are those smirks on their faces?*

Sharp—shooting guard Jason Bragg glowered at Smith and Jury from his place in the lay-up line. *We're about to get it shoved to us again.* Bragg, it turned out, was psychic.

Ironically, when Butler began coaching at VVHS in the 1960s, he thought Smith and Jury were the best tandem of officials in the referee's entire association. Over the years though, his opinion had metamorphosed into something even Kafka would have detested. Jury and Smith had become prejudiced against VVHS, Butler was sure of it. Perhaps it was Butler's abrasiveness that had turned Smith and Jury against him. Butler was forever a psychological wizard inside referees' heads. Perhaps Smith and Jury had grown weary of Butler's spells and had taken on a personal mission of showing Butler they could no longer be psychologically manipulated. Butler felt as far back as the late 1970s that Smith and Jury were making biased calls just to spite him and by the late 1980s Butler held the opinion that Smith and Jury were egotistical jerks who loved the power that their referee stripes and whistles gave them whenever they stepped on to the court. Butler was not the only coach who felt this way about them.

To corroborate Butler's impressions that Smith and Jury put out nefarious vibes whenever they appeared together to officiate, in 1988 a cadre of teams from the San Andreas and Sunkist leagues petitioned to have Smith and Jury blackballed from assignments to any of their league games; unfortunately the vote among athletic directors fell one short. I, too, personally attended games in the 1980s where Smith and Jury officiated and found their attitudes to be arrogant and condescending. More recently, at a high school playoff game in 2002 between Silverado of Victorville and Yucaipa, I heard a disgruntled Yucaipa fan call out to the referees from the stands to berate a bad call, "Who are you guys anyway, Smith and Jury?"

As Victor Valley took the court against Damien, Butler thought about his Achilles' heel, his short temper with officials. The polarity between him, Smith and Jury wouldn't do his Rabbits any good. Tonight he would maintain his composure no matter what they pulled.

Everyone who knows sports knows the best coaches are always master psychologists too. That moniker had long been applied to Butler. As a coach, Butler strategically used psychology to motivate his players. Don Wilson, a former head football coach and teaching colleague of Butler's at VVHS for many years, confirms that Butler was a genius at inspiring his players while simultaneously working the officials. "Butler was a great baiter, but he always knew his limit. He took a lot of pressure off his teams that way."

Often Butler would purposely draw a technical foul then take a time-out. He'd chew his players out for losing their focus, point to the fact that he'd just gotten a technical foul fighting for them, then challenge them to do something for themselves. Nine times out of ten the Rabbits would return to the court following Butler's technical and follow-up time-out with jump-started engines, often running off four or five straight steals and baskets. Tonight though, Butler knew better than to use this strategy. He wasn't going to bait Smith and Jury. He was going to keep his mouth shut. *But who would do the talking then?*

If you go back and talk to any player who ever played for Ollie Butler, they will all tell you the same thing. Butler did not allow his players to argue with or verbally abuse the referees, no matter how badly the game was called, period. Butler handled the officials. He relished the job. Any player who argued with the officials besides the team captain would find himself next to Butler on the bench. The Jackrabbits were known as a disciplined program. But this game was an anomaly. From the beginning to the end there was tense friction between the VVHS players and the refs, a carryover from the Cajon game two nights before, and fans and observers say Butler didn't check it as he normally would have. Why not? Because he had his own personal war going on with Smith and Jury, who tonight would transgress all the bounds of professional decorum in regards to officiating.

Throughout the game between VVHS and Damien both fans and players claimed that Smith and Jury "dissed" Butler—to use the parlance of the streets at the time ("dissing" means disrespecting). Victor Valley High School District Board President at the time, Mike Davis, said that fellow board member Jack Wedgewood was at the game and told him later that he and other fans heard Jury say at various times throughout the game, "Sit down old man!" or worse, "Shut up old man!" They said Jury also directed the "N" word at some of Victor Valley's African American players. Butler, despite his goal of keeping his mouth shut to avoid alienating the refs, could not keep quiet like he intended and once the antagonism got rolling it escalated beyond any tension Butler had ever experienced between himself and officials in his entire career. No longer was the badinage a good-natured part of the game, it had become personal. And when his players took up for him against Smith and Jury, Butler did not protest their support.

As the game progressed, the verbiage between Butler and the refs increased, so did the talk between the Victor Valley players and the refs. Fans taunted Smith and Jury too—but there was nothing abnormal about that. Midway through the second half it felt like the house was about to catch fire. Then, late in the fourth quarter, the smoldering kindling exploded.

With the score tied 51-51, and one second remaining on the game clock, VVHS had the ball out of bounds under their own basket with a chance for one last shot to win the game. Butler set up an in-bound play designed to go to Thomas Wilkins who was having a pretty good offensive game. The inbound passer slapped the ball to signal the start of the play. Slap… Spin… Motion…Whir…

WHISTLE!

On the video-tape viewed at the CIF inquest, a minor push-off by Thomas Wilkins was detected as the Rabbits tried to inbound the ball. It was a non-flagrant foul that seldom gets called, especially that late in the game. Most referees would rather have the players decide the game than have their whistles do so. But this was Dick Smith and Al Jury officiating. They didn't like Butler or his Rabbits and they had no qualms about blowing their whistles with one second to go. They'd done nearly the same thing two nights ago at Yucaipa and it cost the Rabbits a tournament championship. It looked like they were pulling the same stunt tonight.

With a foul called on Wilkins, possession went to Damien and Ken Morrison went to the free throw line to shoot a one-and-one foul shot. All he needed to do was make one and VVHS would go home losers. But the CIF officials weren't viewing the video-tape made by a Damien parent to see if the referees were justified in making their call, they were viewing the tape to see what happened after the call was made.

According to newspaper accounts, the videotape showed that as the players from both teams walked down court from the Victor basket to the Damien basket after the foul was called on Wilkins, Victor Valley's Carlton Hyder and referee Al Jury exchanged what appeared to be heated words. When they lined up at the Damien free-throw line the video showed Jury still mouthing angry looking words in the direction of Hyder and Wilkins. After Morrison shot and made his first free throw, Jason Bragg crossed the lane to change rebounding positions and he, too, was seen exchanging verbal jibes with Jury. Bragg admitted that he, Wilkins and Hyder were all riding Jury about his foul call. When Morrison hit his second shot it was all but over for Victor. With two seconds still remaining on the game clock they in-bounded the ball and heaved it toward their basket 94 feet away. The desperation shot didn't come close.

Not surprisingly, the Victor Valley players and fans were irate and so was Butler. He was livid. For the second game in a row, at least it seemed that way to them, referees Smith and Jury had purposely stolen their chance to win fairly with controversial calls. On top of that, Smith and Jury had verbally abused Butler throughout the game. Officials have every right to tell a coach to sit down and be quiet, but to say "Sit down old man" or "Shut up old man" was plain impudent.

Butler's players were too loyal to him to allow Smith and Jury to get off the hook without hearing what they had to say. Butler felt the same way but he was controlling his anger. He was afraid of what would happen if he got into it with Smith and Jury. *Better settle down first.* Maybe he'd file a grievance tomorrow. Seething, he strode to the opposing bench, congratulated and shook hands with Damien's coach, then proceeded on into the locker room to cool off.

Jackson Wong, the freshman coach who was filling in as Butler's assistant for Willie McDonald (whose JV team was playing in a tournament elsewhere), directed the Rabbit players through the obligatory single-file sportsmanship handshake line as Butler proceeded into the locker room. But Wong, unused to the varsity routine that Butler and McDonald had established regarding player supervision after a game on the road, drifted away from the players over to the scorer's table to collect the stat book and stat girls. That's when the players got out of hand. Had Wong not turned his back to the floor, and had Butler remained in the gym until his players were all in the locker room, perhaps things would have worked out differently; but that's something we'll never know. What happened, happened, and it can't be undone by second guesses.

In a game like basketball, common sense dictates that if a referee's whistle decides the outcome of a tight game in the final seconds, the players on the losing team aren't going to be happy about it. They will undoubtedly get riled up, and it will be worse if they believe the referees purposely sabotaged the game. It's the nature of men to feel their manhood challenged in this sort of situation, and with sports simulating the battlefield athletes can be expected to act like warriors. Being vanquished is hard enough to accept but being cheated is an entirely different matter. The hormone-pumping-testosterone-machines embodied in the 16 and 17 year old Jackrabbits just couldn't stand it and what happened next in the Moreno Valley High School gym should come as no surprise to people who understand young men, competition and unfairly wielded authority. It is history that will be repeated if we forget it.

While Wong was at the score table, Carlton Hyder and Thomas Wilkins drifted toward Al Jury, who had not yet left the court. They lambasted him about his late foul call. Jury, whose day job was a CHP officer, took exception to their accusations. According to witnesses he pushed Carlton Hyder away from him and called him a "country nigger" as he did so. The videotape made by Damien fans apparently missed this when it panned to the scoreboard, but when the camera returned to the floor it reportedly caught Hyder responding with a round-house punch to Jury's jaw. Thomas Wilkins let a punch fly too. With that, all hell broke loose. Parents, fans, players, school staff and security whirled around like a Texas tornado.

Meanwhile, at about the same time toward mid-court, Dick Smith had been corralled by other angry Victor Valley players. Their voices had reached fever pitch, and Butler, who heard the commotion from the locker room raced back into the gym to find an overwhelmed Wong struggling to settle things down. In a split second, Butler saw his players around Smith, so he ran to them at mid-court intending to deescalate the situation. But by the time he skidded to a stop it was way too late for that.

Smith dropped into a boxer's stance as Butler arrived, prancing a-la-Muhammad Ali, and began baiting Butler. "Come on old man! Let's go at it! I'll whip your ass!"

Butler, dismayed, backed up with his arms spread wide to push back his players. He had no inclination to fight a referee. He was trying to restore the peace, but Mike Butler didn't know that. From his vantage point near the Jury-Hyder-Wilkins brawl, where he was trying to pull Carlton Hyder away from Jury, it looked like Smith, who was advancing toward his dad, was about to attack. Mike let go of Hyder and charged to his dad's rescue. That's when destiny dealt a cruel blow to Ollie and Michael Butler, changing the direction of their lives forever.

Mike rushed in at Smith unseen from a side angle, swinging wildly. One glancing blow knocked Smith backwards, stunning him. Butler instinctively grabbed Mike, spun him away from Smith, and dragged him in the opposite direction just as Moreno Valley High administration and security finally intervened. Cooler heads prevailed and the riotous atmosphere was quelled. Victor Valley was escorted to their locker room. The altercation was over but the aftermath was only beginning.

Butler got his players home safely that night, but not before Victor Valley principal Julian Weaver had been phoned at home by friends and given a preliminary account of the melee. The next day a CIF investigation began.

The first thing Julian Weaver did when he arrived at school the next morning was to contact Riverside Tournament officials for more information. After their discussion it was mutually agreed that Victor Valley would withdraw from the remainder of the tournament. Next, Weaver called Butler into his office to hear his side of the story. Butler explained what happened and why he happened to be in the locker room rather than supervising his players. He explained he was trying to stay clear of Smith and Jury himself, and that it was customary for his assistant coach (normally Willie McDonald) to clear the bench and make sure all the players and equipment made it into the locker room, that was why he wasn't on the floor when the scuffle broke out. He had taken for granted that assistant coach Wong would perform the same duties as Willie McDonald always had. Weaver was not satisfied with Butler's explanation. He suspended him, effective immediately, for supervisorial neglect, and suspended the players involved in the physical and verbal altercation from school for five days as well.

This was only the second time in 35 years of coaching that Butler had been suspended. His first suspension came from Weaver too. Two years earlier, Butler exceeded his authority by pulling rank on the girl's basketball coach, tossing her and her mediocre team out of the gym so his boys could practice for the CIF playoffs. A clear violation of Title 9, Weaver dealt severely with Butler on that score by suspending him for the first three weeks of the 1988-89 season, and warned him that more serious consequences would follow if Butler got out of line again. Weaver was unhappy with Butler's attitude. He said, "Butler had become too big. That he had an aura of invincibility around him. He was not contrite. He was just like Bobby Knight."

Since then, rumors have circulated that Weaver held a grudge against Butler that ran deep. Weaver denies those rumors. As an outstanding student-athlete at VVHS in the 1960s, he earned a scholarship to play football and baseball at Cal Western and had impressive grades to go along with his athleticism. He also played basketball in Butler's program through his junior year. As a senior, one rumor went, Butler cut Weaver following varsity tryouts and that's what began their legendary animosity. Weaver doesn't remember it that way. "As I recall, I realized my senior year that my sports future was in football and baseball so I didn't even go out for basketball. I don't know who made up that story that Butler cut me. If it was Butler, I would be very hurt."

Weaver denies any grudge, saying that Butler was one of his main inspirations in high school. He had Butler for his history teacher and admired him for delving into what the textbook left out. It was during the height of the Civil Rights Movement when Weaver had Butler's class. Butler extolled Martin Luther King Jr.'s nonviolent principals. He held lengthy class discussions about the nation's long oppression of Blacks in America. He encouraged young African Americans to take college prep courses so they could go on to college and get educated so they would be able to help plot a course for making much needed social improvements in the area of racial discrimination. Weaver, of African American descent, says he always admired Butler's teaching and his coaching, and that if you walk into his house today one of the pictures in his foyer—where he displays photographs of his role models—is of Ollie Butler.

Even so, as principal of Victor Valley High Weaver was Butler's boss and had inherited the unenviable task of supervising the intense Butler and his basketball program, that is where he says their friction first developed. As principals Gunn and Conde had done before Weaver, he had to deal with the complaints that crossed his desk regarding Butler's animated courtside behavior, which some people took offense to. Don Conde, who was assistant principal at VVHS from 1967-71 and principal from 1971-81 (and interim principal again in 2000), says that his own observation of Butler at games would occasionally prompt him to call Butler into his office for a talk. Though Conde would not discuss what was said in their private meetings, he acknowledged over the years letters were placed in Butler's confidential personnel file regarding matters related to basketball. He also believed that Weaver had that file opened in Executive Session with the School Board of Trustees when he tried to get Butler fired. It never came to anything close to that with Conde in charge, he and Butler always worked things out. Conde added that, "Ollie Butler was the best high school basketball coach I ever saw in all my years as principal, and I saw a lot of them as I never missed a game, home or away, in all those years."

As principal, Weaver was in a tough place regarding this incident. Like Conde and Gunn he admired Butler's coaching. "Ollie Butler was an outstanding coach," Weaver said. "His tactical knowledge and preparation was excellent." Unfortunately, Weaver thought Butler's temperament had become hostile. "I was worried he was becoming a negative role model." Weaver had warned Butler when he suspended him for usurping the girl's coach practice time, that any further inappropriate behavior would not be condoned. Now this. Weaver's reputation was on the line. But how do you fairly discipline your own former teacher and coach, a guy who is a legend in his own time? Yet, if it was any other coach whose players hit officials, he knew what the answer would be. He had no other choice, Butler had to go.

To Weaver the evidence was clear. It was a matter of doing what he felt was right. He urged the Superintendent, George Davis, to fire Butler. The videotape made by Damien High School parents was offered into evidence. The tape, which Weaver says Butler refused to watch, clearly showed Carlton Hyder, Thomas Wilkins and Michael Butler all take swings at Smith and Jury. "Butler, as head coach, was ultimately responsible for his players actions," said Weaver.

Assistant coach Jackson Wong reviewed the tape along with Weaver and other VVHS administrators as well as the School Board. He confirms these details but adds that the tape also showed Smith and Jury antagonizing the Victor Valley players prior to the fisticuffs. Still, Weaver felt the referees' behavior did not justify the player's reactions or Butler's lack of supervision.

The official CIF investigation resulted in Mike Butler and Thomas Wilkins being hit with the CIF "Death Penalty." This rule, rarely invoked, addresses players assaulting referees. Carlton Hyder was also given the "Death Penalty" but with a proviso. Since he was pushed away by Al Jury, his retaliatory punch mitigated the assault charge against him. In September his case would be reviewed and he could be reinstated by the CIF if he met the provisions assigned. (He did and was reinstated to the basketball program for his senior year.) Jason Bragg, Victor Valley's captain, was put on probation for the remainder of his senior year for his verbal assault of the officials, though he had not been involved in any physical altercation. If he even got a technical foul he would also be removed from the team. In the mean time, the three "Death penalty" recipients were banned from playing any competitive high school sports again, and immediately dropped from the 1989-90 team, all the way down to having their names expunged from the already printed programs.

The CIF, however, did not take any disciplinary action against Ollie Butler, which posed a problem for Weaver. Superintendent George Davis, who Weaver had petitioned to fire Butler, had no support from the new school board. A majority of new members had been voted in following the strike in 1985 and they did not appreciate Davis's attempt to run the district like a dictator. Realizing that Butler loyalists on the School Board, two of whom who were at the game and personally witnessed Smith and Jury baiting Butler and the VVHS players, would not support a decision to terminate Butler, Weaver had no choice but to back down and reinstate Butler as head coach. Weaver was so upset when the Board would not back him that he stormed out of the meeting saying, "I guess Ollie Butler is God around here." With no support from School Board, both Superintendent Davis and Principal Weaver resigned at the end of the year.

As it turned out, this decision advanced Weaver's career quite a bit. In July of 1990, he was hired by a school district in Davis, California, not long after he turned in his resignation at Victor Valley. They were looking for a principal who wasn't afraid to take on the "good old boy" network entrenched in their particular area. Someone on the interview panel had heard about Weaver's attempt to fire a legendary coach. In discussing the incident in the interview, it was apparent to them that Weaver was the guy they needed to take on their own problematic personnel. Weaver spent three years in northern California playing head roller, then parlayed his professional advancement into a high powered position with the San Bernardino County superintendent's office, where today he has risen to the number two position. "If I hadn't gone through all of that back in 1989-90 I never would have achieved what I have," Weaver said. "I would probably still be the principal at Victor Valley. I really did love that job and planned to stay in it until I retired."

After all you've heard, you might wonder if anything happened to the two officials involved in this incident? They had been rude and unprofessional badgers during the fateful game. They had antagonized Victor Valley players, coaches, and fans. One of them had even pushed a player. Were they disciplined in any way? Ultimately not. They got a little bad press and presumably a behind closed doors slap on the hand, but the vote to officially reprimand them fell short, due, cynics believe, to their inside connections with CIF commissioners.

Victor Valley High was embarrassed by the scandal and Ollie Butler was personally devastated. He believed that Smith and Jury were the real culprits in the whole affair and he was disgusted that they had escaped punishment while three key players—two of them expected to go on to play college ball—had their high school basketball careers ruined. More importantly, he was worried about his son Mike.

As a junior, Mike had another year to go. Butler had already planned to retire at the end of Mike's senior year. Now he wondered if Mike would even make it through the eleventh grade. Basketball had helped Mike deal with his sister's death the same way it had his father, by providing an energy releasing distraction. Without basketball, Mike was quickly slipping back into that familiar depression, though much deeper now than ever before because he had the weight of besmirching his father's reputation with his assault on Dick Smith. Some critics were saying Butler had gotten lax in his discipline of his players in the latter Eighties, and that this incident proved it. He couldn't even control his own son, they said.

Ollie Butler, on the other hand, couldn't have been prouder of Mike. What father could be upset with a boy who had perceived a threat to his dad and come to the rescue? Remember, Mike thought Smith was about to attack his dad. So did a lot of other people. Sure, Butler wished Mike hadn't been so impulsive, but he could easily understand his son's reaction. Mike wishes he hadn't been so impulsive that night, too. "I'd never even been in a fight before," he said. "I'd never done anything like that. I just lost my head."

There was a brief period of time there just after the investigation concluded when Butler felt like quitting and staying home with Mike after school, but he knew that wasn't the right thing to do. He had a job to finish, something he learned from his father as a boy that one must always do, finish what you start no matter how difficult it becomes. He needed Mike to see him meet this challenge. One had to be resilient in life. Quitting wasn't an option in the Butler household. So Butler returned to the gym and relieved Willie McDonald who had acted as interim head coach during his suspension.

The team languished for a while, but by mid-season Butler had them back in the running for the title, though they had to settle for second place in the end. But in the playoffs they made some noise in the first round when they knocked off the highly regarded 19-6 West Covina Bulldogs, champions of the Sierra League. Jason Bragg's hit a 3-pointer at the end of regulation to tie the game and send it into overtime, where VVHS prevailed.

This gave Butler his 605th career win. It was also his last win. The Rabbits lost their second round game and Butler's resignation followed soon after.

Butler might have stayed on through Mike's senior year, his family wanted him to. But as the 1989-90 season drew to a close, pugilistic referee, Dick Smith, who was also the assigner for the Inland Empire Basketball Officials Association, vindictively cooked up a scheme to see to it that Butler was forced out at Victor Valley. He convinced a majority of the officials in the IEBOA to vote to boycott all Victor Valley High School athletic contests—meaning all sports—if Ollie Butler remained the head basketball coach. Smith convinced his minions that none of them were safe in hostile Victor Valley territory as long as the wild-man Butler was permitted to remain. What kind of a school district could allow a coach to retain his job after his players had assaulted referees? Smith maligned all of Victor Valley's sports programs. To him, Victor Valley was an out of control ghetto school, a proven threat to any official, and a danger to opposing schools' players and fans.

Butler could again read the writing on the wall but this time it didn't take a Daniel to decode the message. If his resignation would keep the officials from boycotting Victor Valley games, then that's what he had to do. This was a battle he couldn't win. Besides, with his son Mike's hoop dreams crushed, his heart was no longer in his coaching. Both their dreams were dead. It was a rotten way to end an era of 28 seasons at Victor Valley High School.

RETIREMENT

In 1994, a huge retirement party was held at the Holiday Inn in Victorville to celebrate Butler's career. Players came from each decade Butler coached. I was there with many of my Class of '75 teammates. What a spectacle it was to see so many of Butler's former players and students, neighbors, friends and family members gathered together to applaud his influential life. Speeches were given, toasts and roasts made, and games both won and lost were reminisced about. After Bob Jones spoke, Butler consoled him again for probably the hundredth time with, "It's okay Bob, we wouldn't have been there without you." This in reference to Jones tipping in the winning basket for Servite in the 1965 CIF playoffs. (If only I would have had the idea to write a book about Butler's life back then; I could have gathered a lot of quality anecdotes from that bunch.)

After resigning as head basketball coach at Victor Valley following the scandal-marred 1989-90 season, Butler was immediately hired as an assistant coach by Reggie Smith at California State University in San Bernardino. He coached the Coyotes with Smith for three years and when Smith moved on Butler was offered the head coach job in 1994. It was at least the 20th unsolicited college offer he'd had in the last twenty years. He turned the offer down just as he had in the past and elected to hang up his whistle. He'd already planned to retire from classroom teaching at the end of the 1993-94 school year, and basketball had always been another class he taught; he figured he might as well give it all up at once. He was 64 and had achieved every coaching goal he'd set for himself: he'd won over 500 games, won seven out of every ten ball games he'd coached and kept a single varsity program going for over 25 years. To add to his basketball accomplishments, Butler also won Victor Valley High School's coveted Golden Apple award as the Teacher of the Year in 1994.

Since his retirement Ollie Butler has kept busy. As I write, he is in Breckinridge, Colorado, where he and Sharon spend every summer. They have a condominium there. It's not too far from the Denver area where two of their three children now live. Mike is a Parks and Recreation supervisor. He has come a long way since the 11th grade. His parents are very proud of him. Jana is a middle-school teacher, her husband Jeff works for a local municipality, and they have two children: Fharon and Paige. Ollie and Sharon visit them frequently while they are in Colorado during July and August. You would think they'd see their other daughter, Cathy, a lot more often since she lives in Pasadena, but they don't. Cathy, who is working on her Master's degree at UCLA as a museum curator, cannot stomach the lack of culture in the High Desert. If they are to see her with any frequency, they must drive into the city. Going into the city is not their favorite thing to do, but it's not because they don't like to travel.

Ollie and Sharon try to do as much traveling throughout the year as they can. Sharon hasn't retired from teaching quite yet (she teaches third grade at Rio Vista Elementary in Apple Valley, California), but during the winter and spring holidays she and Ollie will either take a European tour or a trip somewhere in the States that they haven't been to yet. Both are avid history buffs, so their trips are not only entertaining, they are educational as well. Do I hear tax write-off?

During the school year while Sharon is working, Ollie has a variety of activities that keep him both mentally and physically sharp. He works outs at Gold's Gym, tutors college students, consults on the school's expulsion board, mentors young coaches and does guest speaking at basketball camps and on rare occasions substitute teaches. I won't mention his more mundane activities: the vacuuming, laundry and dishwashing duties he has taken over, or his old responsibility of mowing the lawn with his reliable push-mower.

Butler works out at Gold's Gym anywhere from three to five times a week. You would never know he's in his seventies or that he has a heart condition. However, it isn't all work-out and no play. Loretta Alvarado, a former student and wife of Henry the Hawk Alvarado of Butler's 1973 and '74 teams, who also works out at Gold's, likes to tease Butler by saying, "he spends more time talking than he does pumping iron." But a lot of that talk isn't just idle chatter. Butler has become acquainted with a lot of young college students at the gym and some of them have talked him into tutoring them.

Depending on the time of year, Butler has anywhere from two to five students who he gives English, history and political science lessons to. He proofreads and edits papers for them, too, and sometimes he even has occasional newcomers to America who he helps with their citizenship studies. His wife mentions that some of his students are awfully young and pretty, but the truth is he works just as hard with Ahmed from Indonesia as he does with Sabrina the former modeling school dropout who is back at the junior college working toward becoming a primary grade teacher.

Butler is also in demand among younger coaches. He will frequently get a phone call from a novice coach who wants to consult with him about basketball practice plans or game strategies or skill drills. Butler never turns down a request from a fellow coach for tips on the game. He is also a favored speaker at summer camps. Kurt Herbst, who succeeded Butler at Victor Valley High School before starting up the basketball program at Victorville's newest high school, Silverado, runs the Victor Valley Basketball Camp for boys and girls ages 8-14. Butler has been a regular

149

DAVID KNISS

speaker at this camp for the past twelve years. One time he might teach shooting, another time defense, or he may just talk about the importance of education. Herbst gives him complete freedom to pick his own topic and Butler never fails to deliver a quality performance—especially if he demonstrates his eyes closed free throw technique. Since Butler's retirement in 1994 he has also helped a number of his former players with their basketball teams. He is the proverbial coach who has forgotten more about the game than most of us will ever know.

Butler is also a member of the Victor Valley High School District's Expulsion Review Board. Students who must go before the Board for some grievous infraction of the rules probably don't know it, but Butler is their best advocate. In his many years in education he's seen it all. He knows kids make mistakes. He knows that youth is the time for experimentation. Adolescent psychology is an avocation with him. If there is any way to give a kid a second or third chance, he will recommend it. Many a student has had his or her educational future salvaged by Butler's vote to give them a stay of expulsion (meaning they get one last chance to make good).

On rare occasion Butler will also make a classroom appearance, filling in for a fellow colleague out for the day at a conference or attending to other school or personal business. He's pretty picky about who he will substitute for though, usually he'll only take the classes of his former history department members, but occasionally he can be talked into substituting for an English teacher. He took my American Literature class for me a few times. He was great. He said I didn't need to make a formal lesson plan for him, just tell him about the book we were reading and when it was set in history, he'd talk to the kids about the historical context of the book. (I can only hope that when I get to be his age I have acquired a fraction of his vast knowledge of American history.)

Butler finally gave up his weekly 3-on-3 game. When he turned 70 he decided he didn't want to chase the youngsters in their forties and fifties around any more. Occasionally though, he will use his own personal key to the Keith Gunn Gymnasium to go in and shoot around. He also likes to help out Matt Denny, Victor Valley's current head coach, by giving his players one on one instruction in shooting.

Another of Butler's favorite diversions in retirement in keeping up on the high school basketball scene. From the first games in late November through the CIF finals in March, if there is a game worth seeing in the area, you can be sure Butler will be there. What makes Butler's presence at these games fascinating is the gathering of the faithful around him. Former players, former and current coaches, parents, school administrators and former colleagues not yet fortunate enough to have retired, will seek Butler out to enjoy the game with, knowing his commentary will be more incisive

150

and colorful than any play by play man you might hear on TV. His knowledge and understanding of the subtleties of the game are encyclopedic, that's why people would rather sit with him than anyone else. Besides that, he's mellowed. He won't rant and rave like some former coaches will, although he did get pretty animated at an overtime game between his old Jackrabbits and their newest rival, Silverado, under Kurt Herbst. He apologized to Matt Denny later for sending down unsolicited advice on what to do—as in put the senior point guard back in and take out the freshman gunslinger in the overtime period—he just got a little carried away.

Which is why I have to end this book with a final chapter on coaching.

DAVID KNISS

ON COACHING

Thomas Carlyle, the Nineteenth Century Scottish essayist, historian, and moralist, said in his "Essay on Burns," that a biography should answer two questions: (1) What and how produced was the effect of society on the man? (2) What and how produced was his effect on society? In the earlier part of this sketch I attempted to establish the effects of society on Ollie Butler. Now, here at the end, I'd like to summarize how Butler effected society.

To Southern California high school basketball fans, Ollie Butler is a coaching legend. He is San Bernardino County's winningest coach with 605 wins against 251 losses—that's winning seven out of every ten games. (And by the way, San Bernardino County is the largest county in the entire nation—bigger than some New England states.) Butler is also one of the winningest high school coaches in the entire country. If he had coached his whole career at a Catholic high school, where he could recruit and hand out scholarships like DeMatha's Morgan Wootten or Mater Dei's Gary McKnight, he probably would have won 1000 games. But a won / lost record shouldn't be the only measure society uses to judge a coach by.

More than teaching basketball players how to be winners, I think one of Butler's greatest contributions to society was his positive influence on his players' characters. As a teacher you normally get a student for one year only but with basketball players it's different. Butler spent a lot more time with the players than with his classroom students, what with two hour practices, long distance bus trips, weekend tournaments, summer league-games and the like. During three years in his program (four years beginning in the mid-Eighties when VVHS became a four year high school), he couldn't help getting close to his players; and during that time, like a watchful guardian, he taught them what they needed to know to achieve prosperity as adults.

In the classroom though, Butler made his mark, too. To him, teaching and coaching were synonymous. He taught his basketball players and he coached his history students. Turn it around and it amounts to the same thing. His direct influence on between 150-200 academic students per year for 32 years still effects society today. Although he taught science and driver's training early in his career, he spent the majority of his years teaching history at Victor Valley High, where it is estimated he taught 4,500 students their American history. Educational researchers have calculated that a classroom teacher with five classes of 35 students per class makes an average of 10,000 interpersonal transactions per day. That's a lot of connecting with kids. In Butler's class, the majority of those interactions

152

were friendly, positive and humorous. Kids leaving Butler's class after a year of positive learning passed that energy on. That's how culture works. We pick up a little here, a little there, we modify it and we pass it on. The more our lives are impacted by positive people, the more likely the future will be effected for the good.

Philosophically, Butler felt it was his job to get his students through their compulsory high school education, rather than hinder them from moving on. He wasn't a "hard-nose." He wasn't unreasonable. He wasn't overly strict. He didn't overwhelm kids. He also wasn't boring. He was the kind of teacher every student likes: energetic, garrulous, entertaining, humorous, light-hearted, yet, someone who also got you thinking.

Butler had a scholar's approach to teaching history. He studied relentlessly. He did his homework. In his early years he often stayed up until 2:00 a.m. reading ancillary material he could incorporate into his lesson plans. He also sought out supplemental materials to use as a break from the dull textbook. His specialty was making frequent connections between current events and those of the past. (I still remember his comparison of the Revolutionary War to the Vietnam War. I think it made such a big impact on me because I was worried about being drafted when I graduated and I didn't want to end up like those Redcoats or like our own Viet Nam vets.) More than anything else, Butler constantly clued his classes into the fact that there was more to history than the abridged version in their School Board approved textbook. "History is written by the winners," he used to say. "But what about the loser's side of the story?" If we really wanted to find out, there was only one way. Butler promoted outside reading as the best way for students to truly educate themselves. He often said, "You can't rely solely on your teachers." In essence, Butler instilled in his history students the same fundamentals for success he inculcated to his players in the gym.

"Overall," Butler said, "I was reasonable in my expectations, didn't overburden the students with homework and tried to make the projects I assigned relevant." In 32 years he only wrote six referrals, proving he knew how to get along with teenagers and how to motivate them. Don Conde, the principal at VVHS between 1971-81, said, "Ollie Butler was a tremendous teacher. He was every bit as good a teacher in his classroom as he was a coach in the gym. His lesson plans were detailed and meaningful, and he had a great delivery."

Beyond history facts and basketball techniques, Butler taught his students and players a more valuable curriculum—good personal work habits. Butler believed that punctuality, proper behavior, the right attire, preparation, commitment, diligence, hard work, relentlessness, teamwork and perseverance would make his players and students successful and productive citizens. He worked these subtle points into the curriculum every day and over time they became as much a second nature to his players and students as the basketball skills he taught or the history facts he ingrained. Butler practiced what he preached, too, he was no hypocrite; though I would be remiss in balanced reporting if I didn't cite the odd occasion when a disparity between Butler's words and his actions came up.

Pat Brannon, who graduated from VVHS in 1975 and later became a teacher and a coach, remembered a time when Butler did not live up to his own teachings. Brannon laughed when he told me about visiting the gym as an eighth grader in the summer of 1971 to play basketball: "Butler sat all of us boys against the wall and gave us a speech about proper sportsmanship, and not cursing, swearing, or fighting. A little later, while I was playing on the far court, I heard Butler yelling at some of the players he was playing against. When his team lost he threw the basketball in disgust to the other end of the gym—but he didn't cuss or swear."

Well, everyone's entitled to an off day. Normally Butler practiced what he preached.

Another contribution to society that many of us took away from our time with Butler was his stress on clean-living. We may not have lived up to his standards then, but I think most of us, when we matured, realized he was right about not "dissipating"—as he was fond of calling any vice potentially harmful to the body.

Butler was pretty pragmatic in his expectations of his players. While he took the high road himself in modeling a healthy lifestyle: he never smoked or chewed tobacco, didn't cuss or use profanity, didn't treat women disrespectfully, and never drank (not even socially); he knew boys in high school still had to grow into their manhood. Peer pressure, natural curiosity, and temptation lined the path, and Butler knew experimentation was a part of growing up. He understood boys weren't always going to make the right decisions. When we committed our youthful indiscretions he was right there to help us clean up the aftermath. He wasn't a guy to turn his back on people just because they'd committed a foul. He was a teacher first, and well he knew that human nature is such that most people learn more from their failures than they do from their successes. But the same way he got swats for ditching school to see a baseball game, we got our consequences from him too. There was always a price to pay before forgiveness.

To this day, and I've seen it happen, Butler takes the news of someone's fall from grace with a slow, nonjudgmental side-to-side wag of his head that seems to say, *I'm so sorry to hear that.* Never an I-told-you-so kind of person, Butler feels genuinely sorry for those who don't find the right paths in life. Some of his former players have spent time in jail as adults. He never says, "I told you so." He never gives up hope either. Fortunately, human flotsam and jetsam aside, most of Butler's former players and students are success stories.

I think Butler was such a good influence on his players and students because he took his work seriously. He always wanted to be the best in whatever he did and he taught that to be the best you had to work harder than the rest. When he decided to become a coach back in the Fifties, he gave it his all. He taught basketball the same way a teacher would an academic subject. He had the same approach to it as he did to teaching history. Pat Douglass calls him, "a basketball scholar."

While Butler's scholastic approach to basketball was the same as it was to history, he demanded far more of his players than he did his regular education students. Basketball wasn't compulsory, it was optional; therefore, Butler could set much higher standards. If you wanted to play for Butler, you had to be tough in order to measure up. According to Butler's friend Bill Lusk, "Not everyone could play for Butler, he was very demanding."

First, there was the endless running he put his players through. Once, when criticized for running his players too much, Butler's responded, "Heck, they're 16 and 17, they're not supposed to get tired."

Second, there was Butler's picayune attention to detail. Most would call it obsessive. Butler would agree. "You have to be obsessive in order to be successful." Every single practice was scheduled down to the minute. In preseason we often had three hour practices, but once the regular season began we started at 2:00 and ended at 4:00, no earlier, no later. Drills were scheduled successively anywhere from three minutes to five minutes to twenty minutes, each building on the one that preceded it.

Mystifyingly, with all Butler's micromanaging, his practices never got off schedule. Unlike some coaches who yell and scream at players who aren't getting a drill right and make them do it over and over, Butler would not continue running an unsuccessful drill. When it was time to move on to the next activity on the practice plan, we moved on, and that night Butler would strategize how to better teach his players what they couldn't grasp during that day's disastrous drill. He got this from Dean Smith, who at a clinic Butler attended said, "Stick to your practice schedule. Don't run a drill longer because players aren't doing it well."

Believe it or not, the floor was swept in a precise way, too: four passes up and down the floor with the dust mop then over to the side to deposit the accumulated dust, then repeat. After 22 passes the floor was properly dusted. Butler wanted nothing to be haphazard. Either do it the right way or don't do it at all. Usually Butler did it himself. I think it was therapy. He also laundered and folded our uniforms and towels himself rather than let an assistant do it or have the players take them home for their moms to do. We better not come to practice in anything other than the assigned attire either, and we had to wear it the right way. Jerseys were tucked in, we had to wear double socks to prevent blisters, shorts were regulation gray and you'd better not fall down spread eagle and get caught without your jock.

And third, there was Butler's ever critical eye, which allowed no mistake to go uncorrected. Butler followed John Wooden's teaching formula, which I believe Wooden passed on from his old coach, Piggy Lambert, at Purdue. He would show us how to do something, then we imitated what he showed us, he then corrected what we did wrong, and we repeated the skill correctly over and over until it was ingrained. When his whistle blew, we stopped, got corrected, started over. This happened in games the same as it did in practice. Forget about not being embarrassed in front of your family, your girl, or your friends. If you did something wrong, Butler let you know about it, RIGHT NOW, in front of everyone. No exceptions. Fortunately, the correction often times took place on the bench because most of the time you got hooked from the game if you screwed up that obviously.

Butler was an old school coach. You did things his way. His way was the right way. The only thing Butler would allow a player to do his own way was shooting, but that was only on one condition. He wouldn't try and change someone's unorthodox style if they were already a good shooter (Norman Olsen and Oscar Lugo to name a couple), but if you weren't a great shooter using your own technique, you had to learn to shoot his way, which of course was the correct way. Butler never failed to improve a poor shooter's percentage by teaching him proper technique.

Rick Novak, an administrator in the Seventies and Eighties at VVHS, once came in to Don Conde's office after watching Butler teach shooting and said, "Ollie Butler should have been a Marine gunnery sergeant. If he could teach the Marines how to shoot rifles the way he teaches his players how to shoot baskets, they'd never miss their targets."

Even though Butler was an old school disciplinarian coach, he had some liberal quirks. One I remember is that he didn't care if his players had long hair. As a history teacher he understood youth rebellion and shifts in societal mores. Unlike coaches from other sports who used haircuts as a way of bringing players into conformity, Butler did not. "Just don't let it get in your eyes," he'd tell guys like Steve Williams. Williams, who played varsity in 1973-74 and 1974-75, was one of a number of players in the Seventies who wore their hair to their shoulders. Williams kept it out of his eyes with a headband during practice and games. Butler never said a word about his long hair. Best of all, Williams said, "Butler never teased me about it like my dad, who called me "Goldilocks."

Butler was a member of SCIBCA (the Southern California Interscholastic Basketball Coaches Association) for many years, serving terms as both an officer and president. He had many other professional affiliations relating to basketball as well. When Coach of the Year awards were handed out the last 15 years of his career, Butler won nine of them. He was nominated to the Naismith Memorial Basketball Hall of Fame in 1994. In March of 1999 he was inducted into the CIF Southern Section Basketball Hall of Fame at the Arrowhead Pond in Anaheim California in front of 10,000 people there to see the CIF finals. His career spanned four decades, and in that time Butler had 23 All-CIF players and 55 All-Leaguers. Hundreds of his players went on to play college ball at one level or another. Three of his players were drafted into the pros: Greg Hyder (Cincinnati Royals), Jerry Hyder (Denver Nuggets), and Tony Anderson (New Jersey Nets); and Jeff Armstrong played five years professionally in connection with the Harlem Globetrotters.

With all these accomplishments, is there anything we can point to as a single key to Butler's success? Probably not. But there is one word pretty popular in Butler's vocabulary, a word he applied in both the classroom and the gym: fundamentals. Ask any of his former players about Butler and fundamentals will eventually come up. Another word that would come up eventually, too, would be: intensity. Put them together and you have intense-fundamentals. If his success could be boiled down to one concept, that might be about as close as you could get to the secret of Butler's achievement over the years.

Besides Butler's more serious contributions, he also brought some lighter touches into the classroom and the gym through his showmanship. Butler was an entertainer as much as he was a teacher and coach. He was an outstanding actor on the histrionic boards: leading man, director, producer, and primary liaison to the audience in the drama he choreographed. The Victor Valley fans loved him. They came to see him. The opposing fans hated him, but they loved to see him, too. Former head Jackrabbit football coach, Don Wilson, says that "Barstow and Burroughs thrived on booing him. He was the enemy. But they respected him as well because he was such a good coach."

Wilson also says that "A lot of people saw through Ollie's facade," meaning that more astute fans realized a lot of Butler's wild courtside behavior was just part of the show. He gave the crowd their money's worth. In the Sixties and Seventies, before there were so many other forms of entertainment to choose from, high school basketball had a huge following, even at schools where their teams lost most of the time. In Victorville, the Keith Gunn Gymnasium was regularly packed with 800-1000 screaming fans every Tuesday and Friday night. In an article that appeared not too long ago in <u>The Sun</u>, the Keith Gunn Gymnasium was ranked the number one most hostile gym for a visiting team to play in, in all of San Bernardino County, a legacy attributable to Butler's 28 year reign.

Butler's knack for showmanship, coupled with an inherent gift for psychology, made him the master of the "psyche out." He knew how to say just the right thing to coaches or refs to get them doubting themselves. Sometimes he'd throw out a weird offensive play or switch a defense just to shake up the opposing coach. Or maybe he'd quote a rule to a referee straight from the rule book verbatim, down to line, paragraph, page number, chapter and section. His players, naturally, were recipients of his psychological manipulation as well. One familiar Butler ploy used at the beginning of the season was to tell the local news reporter, "I have a terrible problem. The new players are just as good as, or better than the returning lettermen, and I never know who're going to be my starters." This never failed to motivate the entire team.

Butler got an early start learning about basketball, but today no one would guess where that start came from. Give up? Butler began his basketball education reclining on the wood floor of whatever shanty the family happened to be inhabiting at the time listening to broadcasts in the late Thirties and Forties of the Kentucky Wildcats. Southwest Tennessee is not that far from Lexington. Butler was raised on the radio-wave teat of Adolph Rupp, for years college basketball's winningest coach (only recently surpassed by Dean Smith who now holds the collegiate records for the most career wins with 879). Though Butler never ascribed to Rupp's racist ways, he did adopt many of his strategies, one of which was "the best defense is a good offense."

Butler was always an offensive-minded coach, though his Jackrabbits may be better known for their stingy defense. UC Irvine coach, Pat Douglass, believes Butler's teams were so successful because "He taught kids how to shoot."

"If you don't put the ball in the basket," Butler says, "how're you going to win? You have to be able to shoot the basketball."

Butler's teams were good at scoring primarily because their offense was so patient. Butler never wanted his team to rush a shot, rather, they were required to work for a good shot with their passing game (most of Butler's coaching took place before the shot clock was implemented). Butler was a big proponent of the eight-to-ten foot bank shot. He felt is was a higher percentage shot. He taught his players how to aim for the top corner of the square painted on the backboard. If you hit it just right, the ball would kiss the glass there and fall right through the net. They also did a lot of scoring off their rapacious defense. Steals and fast breaks were always characteristic of Butler's Jackrabbits, who pressured relentlessly whether in a press, a match-up zone, or in a man-for-man. They played baseline to baseline defense, their feet moving constantly to stay between their man and the basket.

Besides Adolph Rupp, Butler was influenced by many other great college coaches, though the coach who made the greatest impression on him was John Wooden. In many ways Ollie Butler's teams were a high school mirror-image of Wooden's UCLA teams. Victorville is only 90 miles from UCLA and a nanosecond away by TV. Butler used to attend UCLA practices in the Sixties and early Seventies. He often went to see UCLA games, too. If he couldn't go, he watched them on TV. He still does. Religiously.

Mike Moffett, a businessman who graduated from VVHS in 1971, met John Wooden in the early Nineties at a business dinner where Wooden was the motivational key-note speaker. Moffett was fortunate enough to talk with Wooden for about 20 minutes later that night. When Moffett mentioned he had graduated from Victor Valley High, John Wooden knew right away where that was. "Victorville! Ollie Butler coaches there," Wooden said. "Great coach! Great program!"

Like UCLA, Victor Valley played hard, smart and under control. Butler followed the Wooden philosophy that you had to "get your players to play harder than their players." And like Wooden, Butler believed "you must organize your practices and teach your players the right way," so that in games the right way is second nature.

About the only way VVHS wasn't like UCLA was that Victor Valley never won the CIF championship the way UCLA won 10 NCAA championships under Wooden. And maybe Ollie Butler was a little more animated than Wooden on the sidelines. But sans the big titles, VVHS followed the Wooden school of basketball to the letter. "If you are going to imitate," Butler is fond of saying, "imitate the best."

Other marquee name coaches who had an impact on Butler during his career were: Red Auerbach (though Butler never smoked a cigar in his life), Lute Olsen, Denny Crum, Dean Smith, Jerry Tarkanian, and Bobby Knight, to name some of the more recognizable figures. He met most of these coaches at clinics, others he came to know through reading their books, or later in the technological age, through their teaching videos. Denny Crum came to his house to recruit Tony Anderson. He met Lute Olsen when he came to a VVHS playoff game, though Olsen was actually there to scout a player on the opposing team. Jerry Tarkanian became a friend.

Butler first heard about Tarkanian when Tark coached at Riverside City College. Riverside is only 50 miles from Victorville. Tarkanian won three junior college state titles at RCC. Butler finally met Tarkanian in the Seventies after he'd moved on to Long Beach State via Pasadena City

College. Tark was an advocate of the impenetrable 1-2-2 zone defense and a slow it down offense back then. It worked for Tark, so Butler implemented it in Victorville. For many years VVHS was known for their methodical passing game and their 1-2-2 zone defense.

Butler and Tarkanian became better acquainted in the Eighties when Tark moved on to the University of Nevada at Las Vegas where he regularly hosted practice clinics for coaches. In the glitz of the fast lane in Las Vegas, Tark developed a much quicker game plan than the one he used to promote. Butler made regular trips to UNLV to keep up with developing trends in college basketball, which always trickled down, like Reaganomics, to the high school level.

Kent Crosby, who took over the girls basketball program at Victor Valley High in the mid-Eighties, was astounded when Butler presented him with a personal invitation from Tarkanian to a Runnin' Rebel Practice Clinic in 1986. "Tarkanian and Butler were on the same level," Crosby said. "I felt like I was in the big time. We stood right in the middle of the UNLV practice floor next to Tarkanian as he ran the clinic. While I watched, Butler explained everything to me. I thought I knew basketball before; I realized then how little I really knew standing shoulder to shoulder with those two basketball greats."

Back in the Sixties and early Seventies, before NCAA regulations were tightened, Butler was able to take his players to college practices when the colleges started pre-season in October. He wanted his teams to see what the college environment was like and bring education and basketball together in the imagination of his own players. He hoped to inspire them to new heights of achievement. Butler was able to take his teams to watch both Wooden's UCLA and Tarkanian's Long Beach State practices. Beforehand Butler would show the boys around the campus. "The kids were always in awe," Butler said.

Why wouldn't they be? Some of these kids had never been to the big city, and precious few of them had ever toured a college campus. The atmosphere alone was enough to put a look of wonder on their faces. The grand architecture of the buildings, the ornate shapes and colors of the flora in the gardens, the immenseness of the grounds, and the aura of intelligence in the faces of the students they passed, all combined, undoubtedly, to inspire the players to want to go to college themselves.

Once inside the gym, another form of inspiration took hold. The players observed how either Wooden or Tarkanian, depending on whose practice they were observing, structured their practices, ran their drills, and worked with individual players on their skills. This was a familiar situation that confirmed to the players they were in good hands. Butler's own practices were run like these college practices. Butler knew what he was doing!

From Jerry Tarkanian, Butler picked up more than drills and strategies, he was also influenced by Tark's willingness to take chances on players other schools wouldn't. Wooden was just the opposite on this score. Throughout his career, Tarkanian had made it a practice to give kids with bad grades, kids from adverse backgrounds, and even kids who had brushes with the law a second, third, or even fourth chance to redeem themselves. He saw basketball as an incentive he could use to help turn these young men's lives around; something positive: a chance to attend college, get an education and play ball while doing it. Many of Tarkanian's former players have stated that his belief in them when others had given up was what made the difference in them finishing school, getting their degree, and going on to contribute meaningfully to society.

Butler was a lot like Tarkanian in that he could work with just about any kid and at Victor Valley he was give ample opportunity. Victorville had its fair share of "rounders," to use Butler's jargon from childhood in Tennessee—delinquents who would rather play ball than do schoolwork. Butler talked to these kids at school and encouraged them to try out for the team while at the same time reminding them that in order to make the team they had to maintain a minimum grade point average. Having the head coach single them out and encourage them was often just what these rounders needed. If they made the team, Butler then used the classroom as leverage to get these kids squared away both academically and personally. The rougher kids that Butler was able to influence in this way were his real success stories.

Over the years, Butler gave many boys, who maybe didn't have a good foundation at home, something to strive for. He provided direction, discipline, guidelines, and the sense of belonging each of these boys needed. Yet Butler never took much credit for this type of social service. I could, but I won't, mention any names; that wasn't Butler's way. He was always very discreet about these matters.

Another thing Butler was discreet about was helping out kids whose parents couldn't afford tennis shoes or summer camps. Butler, of course, would never give me information like this. I found out all about this by accident in talking to Butler's friend, Bill Lusk. Lusk told me that Butler would diplomatically seek out service-organizations like the Optimists whenever he came across a hardship case that he couldn't afford to take care of out of his own pocket—which Lusk says Butler did frequently. From the various service-organizations Butler would acquire the necessary funds to buy a player a pair of shoes or pay his way to basketball camp. "Butler kept this very hush-hush," Lusk said. "He never wanted a kid or his family to be embarrassed."

However, don't let me give you a false impression that Butler was some sort of bleeding-heart liberal out to save the rambunctious boys of America from corruption on the streets by involving them in sports. He wasn't a "do-gooder" on a mission. He wasn't a miracle worker either. Butler always had to sense something before he'd put in the extra effort. Boys had to meet him part way. One of his favorite sayings is, "You give me a good kid and I'll give you back a good kid. Send me a punk and I'll send you back a punk. Parents build character. Sports just reinforces it." But if there was a boy Butler could see he might be able to reach through basketball, like Tarkanian he didn't mind taking on the challenge.

Butler's legacy lives on at Victor Valley High School. Since he retired there have been two head coaches in the past 12 years. Kurt Herbst took over for Butler in 1990-91 and ran the program through 1997. In 1997-98, Matt Denny succeeded Herbst. Both count Butler as their biggest supporter.

When Herbst was hired, he knew he had big shoes to fill. He had learned all about Butler's reputation and legacy while working as an assistant coach at Pomona Pitzer for seven years, then as an assistant at Covina for three years. By then Butler was an icon in Southern California; there wasn't a veteran basketball coach who didn't know him. While Herbst was confident he could carry on the great tradition Butler had established, he also knew there would be comparisons between him and Butler that he couldn't do anything about.

"The best part about taking the Victor Valley job," Herbst said, "was that everything was in place. Butler ran a quality program and had developed a great tradition of intense winning basketball. All I had to do was keep it going. But that was the worst part, too, having such a tremendous act to follow."

Herbst inherited ten returning players from the previous 1989-90 scandal-marred season and Butler wanted the best for those players. "Ollie talked to me about the kids," Herbst recalled. "He wanted them to have a great season and he knew that the best thing for them was for me to be successful. He mentored me and was supportive of all I did, even though we didn't have the same philosophy about everything. I don't know how I would have survived that first year if it weren't for Butler's support."

The reality of that tradition hit Herbst after their 1990-91 season opening win against Yucaipa in the Yucaipa Classic Tip-Off Tournament. Yucaipa thought they'd pick up an easy win over VVHS with Butler no longer at the helm. They scheduled Victor Valley as a patsy in the first round. Under Herbst, however, the Rabbits gave up no ground and pulled off the win. Herbst was proud of the accomplishment, but where were the reporters? Up in the stands. They had all rushed up to interview Butler as soon as the game clock wound down. Herbst realized then it would be a long time before he'd emerge from Butler's shadow. Eventually he did.

Herbst continued the winning tradition at Victor Valley. In his six years as head coach he took the Rabbits to the playoffs every time. In 1995-96, the Rabbits won the powerful Citrus Belt League and made it all the way to the CIF finals at the Anaheim Pond, although they lost to Long Beach Jordan after leading 26-21 at halftime. Butler knew how Herbst felt after that game and offered some consoling words.

In 1997, Victorville became a two high school town, and Kurt Herbst transferred from Victor Valley to establish the basketball program at the new high school, Silverado. Matt Denny, a former assistant of Herbst, and the head Victor Valley girl's coach for the past five years, took over the boys program. Denny says, "Butler was just as supportive of me as he was of Kurt. And fortunately," Denny added, "No one ever compared me to Ollie the way they did Kurt."

Denny appreciates Butler's willingness to stay involved with the program. "I've had Butler come in to our practices and talk to the players many times," Denny said. "He always makes time for the kids. He'll also sit down with me and talk X's and O's too, whenever I want to run something by him. He continues to be a great asset to this program."

Denny, like Herbst before him, can't speak highly enough of Butler's professionalism and dedication to the kids. "I want these young kids to know about Ollie Butler and the tradition he built here. Right now I'm working on having the gym floor named after him."

Few people who know Butler have any criticism left. His life stands as a testimony to his commitment to family, education, basketball and kids. He has left his mark. He is a winner. Still, there are those who suggest that as a coach he cannot be considered with the greatest because his teams never won a CIF championship. Those who make such remarks obviously don't know what they are talking about.

First of all, Butler never set a goal of winning a CIF title. Was he afraid of setting a goal he might not achieve? I don't think so. Did he lack faith in his ability to coach small town boys to the highest level of achievement? No way. Simply put, whether a team won or lost a CIF championship was never Butler's gauge for success. His barometer always had to do with heart. Had the players given everything they had to give? Had they striven to do everything they'd been taught to the best of their ability? If they had, the wins would take care of themselves and the losses didn't make much difference. With that standard as a measuring rod, Butler didn't need to set a CIF championship as a goal.

Twice Butler's teams made it to the CIF finals and three times they made it to the semifinals. Those were all great teams. Four of those five teams were expected to win it all; yet, there were many other teams along the way that Butler considered more successful than those, teams that may have finished second or even third in league and then lost their first playoff game. Why did he regard some of those teams so highly? Because they achieved beyond everyone's expectations. They applied the fundamentals he gave them with maximum intensity. A coach can't ask for more than that. Success is measured by heart.

Fundamentals. Intensity. Heart. These are the three words I hope you will take away from this story.

To wrap it up, let me end with an anecdote. Recently, when I was at the donut shop having coffee with some of the regulars and talking about the latest basketball game between Matt Denny's Victor Valley Jackrabbits and cross-town rival Kurt Herbst's Silverado Hawks, Ashley Gatson, a retired school district custodian, put the current scene in perspective, "Yeah, it was a good game, but it's just not like it was when the old master was here," referring of course to Ollie Butler.

Time marches on. Change is constant. Heroes come and heroes go. But the world is always a better place when regular people do extraordinary things. Ollie Butler rose from poverty, served his country, sought education, raised a family, excelled in a noble career and passed on to future generations his passion and his love. He is a fine example of making your life count.

THE END

ABOUT THE AUTHOR

David Kniss is a native Southern Californian who has been writing recreationally for over twenty-five years. He teaches English at Victor Valley High School in Victorville, California, the same high school he graduated from in 1975. He also coaches basketball and is an avid reader.

CPSIA information can be obtained at www.ICGtesting.com
Printed in the USA
BVOW011917150812

297990BV00001B/29/A

9 781403 378606